Managansett Press

Don D'Ammassa is the author of:

Horror
Blood Beast
Servant of Chaos*
Caverns of Chaos*
Wings over Manhattan
The Gargoyle
That Way Madness Lies*
Little Evils*
Passing Death*
Date with the Dark*
The Devil Is in the Details*
Living Things*
Shadows Over R'Lyeh*

Science Fiction
Scarab*
Haven*
Narcissus*
Translation Station
The Sinking Island*
Alien & Otherwise*
Wormdance*
Sandcastles*
Carbon Copies*
Phantom of the Space Opera*

Mysteries
Murder in Silverplate*
Dead of Winter*
Death at the Art Gallery*
Death on the Mountain*
Death on Black Island*

Fantasy
The Kaleidoscope*
Elaborate Lies*
The Maltese Gargoyle*
Perilous Pursuits*
Multiplicity*
The Hippogriff of the Baskervilles*

Nonfiction
The Encyclopedia of Science Fiction
The Encyclopedia of Fantasy and Horror
The Encyclopedia of Adventure Fiction
Masters of Detection Vol I*
Masters of Detection Vol II*
Masters of Detection Vol III*
Architects of Tomorrow Vol I*

*published by Managansett Press

MASTERS OF HORROR VOL I

Copyright ©2016 by Don D'Ammassa. All rights reserved. If you would like to use material from this book other than brief excerpts for review purposes, prior written permission must be received by contacting the author at dondammassa@cox.net.

Managansett Press First Edition 2016

MASTERS OF HORROR VOL I

CONTENTS

Introduction	8
Escaping the Past: George R.R. Martin's *The Armageddon Rag*	10
Ray Cluley's *Probably Monsters*	16
Horror Stories and Other Horror Stories by Robert Boyczuk	21
Susie Moloney's *Things Withered*	26
The Schweitzer Mythos	30
Rick Yancey's Monster Hunters	33
Every House is Haunted by Ian Rogers	43
Three Novels by Eric Red	46
Norman Berrow's *The Ghost House*	53
Two by the Davis Brothers	57
Gertrude Atherton	61
Mrs. H.D. Everett	63
The Aylmer Vance Stories	68
William H. Hallahan	73
Louisa Baldwin	79
Lettice Galbraith	83
In Ghostly Company	87
William Fryer Harvey	91
Mrs. J.H. Riddell	97
Marjorie Bowen/Joseph Shearing	105
Russell Kirk	113
Cody Goodfellow's Mythos	119
Henry S. Whitehead	121
Three Novels of Witchcraft	126
Sarban	132
The John Silence Stories	139
D.K. Broster	145
Amelia B. Edwards	150

R. Murray Gilchrist 155
W.W. Jacobs 158
Edith Nesbit 161

INTRODUCTION

I have loved horror fiction from the time I first read Bram Stoker's *Dracula* at the age of ten until the present. It seems to me the genre which most frequently evokes genuine emotions in the reader. Horror plays on our fear of death and lets us confront it directly rather than through implication. It is not an accident that ghost stories were considered just as worthy as any other form of fiction during the Victorian era, or that contemporary writers like Stephen King, Anne Rice, Peter Straub, and others frequently appea on bestseller lists.

There are different definitions of what horror fiction is. I generally do not consider a story to be horror unless there is some element of the fantastic involved, so *Silence of the Lambs* and other novels of psychological horror don't fit my definition. That isn't to say that they can't be brilliant and horrifying in their own right, but it's a different kind of tension.

Horror stories used to deal with only a few basic premises – ghosts, witchcraft, vampires, werewolves, curses, and possession. While all of these themes have survived into contemporary horror fiction, they have all been changed, in some cases dramatically. The contemporary zombie – which isn't really a zombie in the historical sense – is a kind of amalgamation of vampires and werewolves. Vampires have largely been divorced from their undead origins and are now often presented as romantic figures. Werewolves have become shapechangers – people who become leopards or cats or something other than wolves – and they too have become romanticized. Ghost stories have become relatively rare, perhaps because they don't lend themselves to transformation.

The essays that follow were written over a period of several years and deal primarily with the Victorian era. They vary from analytical to simple surveys of the work of obscure writers to extended book reviews. Many of these authors are so out of fashion that few people are likely to read them today, so this is a quick way to get some idea of their output without actually reading them.

The purpose of horror fiction, just as with any other genre, is to entertain. There is no unifying theme to the essays that follow and they aren't designed to convince you of anything. Hopefully they will prove to be informative. I don't imagine anyone will find them all interesting, but I hope that everyone will find something to like.

Escaping the Past: George R.R. Martin's *The Armageddon Rag*

Writers and film makers have both frequently tried to exploit what is perceived as an affinity between supernatural horror and rock music, rarely with much success. Both tend to be unsettling, disturbing, even rebellious, and both are more likely to appeal to a younger, more restless audience. Hollywood's forays have usually led to disastrous results, with *The Rocky Horror Picture Show* as the only obvious exception. Horror writers have not fared noticeably better. The Shock Rock anthology series only lasted for two volumes and novels like *Stage Fright* by Garrett Boatman, *Rockabilly Hell* by William W. Johnstone, *Big Rock Beat* by Greg Kihn, *Music* by Stephen Smoke, and Somtow Sucharitkul's rock and roll vampire novels have not proved to be lasting successes.

The exception is *The Armageddon Rag* by George R.R. Martin, which first appeared from Poseidon Press in 1983, and which has been reprinted several times since, most recently by Bantam. Martin's success is due in part to the fact that he clearly was not writing a horror novel about rock and roll, or a rock and roll novel that included some horror. He was writing about a period in time and a place in our culture during which music was more than just entertainment; it was also a reflection of what we were and what we hoped to be.

Even before the narrative starts, Martin asserts that we didn't all experience the same past even if we think that's the case. He sets new words to the theme of the television series, *All in the Family*, which nostalgically – and unrealistically – referred to a time when everything seemed simpler and, colored by a disdain for the present, people were happier and life was easier. Martin's version substitutes casual sex, drugs, exotic religions, and a less ordered lifestyle, hinting that while the novel will be in part about what happened during the 1960s, it won't necessarily be the same decade that his readers remember.

The opening scene establishes the fact that people deal with the past in very different ways. Sandy Blair is a freelance writer who formerly worked for *The Hedgehog*, until he was fired because he resisted efforts to cut the magazine's ties with the previous generation's rock music and advocate more trendy, contemporary styles. Although *The Hedgehog* has become much more commercially viable, Blair still resents what he sees as betrayal of the reasons that it was founded in the first place. He reluctantly agrees to write an article about Jamie Lynch, a controversial rock promoter who was murdered in what appears to have been a satanic ritual. From the outset, this decision creates waves in his life. The woman with whom he lives, a realtor, accurately diagnoses his impulsive decision as an attempt to recapture his youth, and she resents it and accuses him of immaturity. This tension between holding onto the past and accepting the present is one of the underlying themes of the novel. Blair recognizes that his view of the world during the 1960s was naïve, but it is that very ingenuousness that makes him so reluctant to let it go.

    In the first chapter we are also introduced to the Nazgul, a rock group whose albums are filled with grotesque images and have titles like *Hot Wind out of Mordor*, *Napalm*, and *Music to Wake the Dead*. It was the last of these albums that was playing when Lynch was murdered, his heart cut out as described in the lyrics of one of the songs. The murder takes place on the thirteenth anniversary of the break-up of the Nazgul (the number is certainly not coincidental) after their lead singer was shot to death by an unknown assassin during a concert in Albuquerque. The dead singer's name was Patrick Henry Hobbins, an obvious reference to Old Hob, a term for the devil, although his nickname was the Hobbit, another Tolkien reference. The Nazgul referred to Lynch, who was their manager, as Sauron because of the draconian measures he took to control them. The names of the other band members may also be significant. Maggio is a term applied to a form of musical ritual thought to be prehistoric in origin. There is even a moment later in the novel when Blair speculates on the significance of names, perhaps hinting that the reader should look below the surface. His own name, Sander, is a diminutive of Alexander, which means "protector of man", a connotation that proves significant late in the novel.

    Blair decides to interview each of the surviving Nazgul, starting with Gopher John Slozewski, who runs a small night club and looks more like a business executive than a rock star. Slozewski is a quiet, undemonstrative, but basically friendly type who is spending his own money to help young musicians get their first break. He tells Blair that Lynch was still contractually the manager of the Nazgul and that this was one of the reasons they'd never reunited, had in fact recently turned down a proposition from another promoter named Edan Morse. That restriction no longer applied now that Lynch was dead, but Slozewski prefers to stay with his club, which becomes a moot point when it mysteriously catches fire, killing scores of people.

Martin quickly moves to dispel any lingering doubt that Blair is embarked on a journey into the past, His next stop is to visit the first woman he ever loved, Maggie Sloane, who still has the same cat, although some parts of her life clearly have changed. It is at this point that Blair realizes that rather than having helped to change the world, he has himself been changed, as has everyone and everything around him. Later he will imagine her telling him that she is "not the girl I was", and indeed none of his college friends are any longer. As he visits each of them during the course of his trip, he discovers that even those who believe they have stepped out of the stream of time are fooling themselves. Bambi lives in a commune and denies that the outside world has any influence, but there are already signs that their community is coming to an end, Lark has become an advertising executive, and Froggy has been forced to give up his theatrically anti-establishment attitude just to survive. "The revolutionaries have bought tract homes and three-piece suits." The most revolutionary of them all, Slum, has been declared incompetent and is held prisoner by his sadistic father.

Blair also discovers that Edan Morse was a significant player in the violent underground of the 1960s, until he was expelled by his associates following his shift from activism to Satanism. He arranges a meeting, openly suspicious that Morse is responsible not only for the murder of Lynch but for the fire at Gopher John's bar. Morse suggests that it may be possible to reverse time after a fashion, to recover the momentum of change that emerged during the 1960s, a tide that ebbed when the Nazgul lost their lead singer to an assassin.

To prove that he is serious about setting the clock back, Morse reveals that he has found a nearly exact replacement for the dead Pat Hobbins and that he does indeed intend to bring back the Nazgul, implying that there are forces bigger than the individuals involved compelling them to reunite. Thanks in part to cosmetic surgery,

Larry Richmond is a dead ringer for the young Pat Hobbins. Blair is also introduced to Morse's two closest associates, Gortney Lyle and Ananda Caine.

Blair begins to experience recurring nightmares of ghastly Nazgul concerts, filled with blood and fear and horrible imagery, intermixed with distorted flashbacks to violent events in the 1960s. Although Blair still believes that the would be promoter is delusional, Caine suggests that the disturbing dreams were a direct result of Morse's supernatural intervention. His disillusionment has been reinforced at every stage of his journey and he feels at times that all the forces of repression are sharing the same face beneath their individual disguises, and that he himself can no longer distinguish between good and evil. His confusion is reinforced by the lyrics of one of the Nazgul's songs, which includes the phrase "right is wrong, black is white". The dichotomy of Blair's feelings is also reflected by the fact that when he begins experiencing nightmares, he names his car "Daydream".

This is the point when Blair begins to wonder whether it might be possible to set time back after all, to change things so that he and his friends turned into the people they wished to be rather than what they are. He experiences an epiphany in which he remembers that Larry Richmond, the new Patrick Henry Hobbins, was born in Bethlehem, Pennsylvania. Christ died for our sins and Patrick Henry died for his country. But is Richmond/Hobbins the Second Coming, or the Anti-Christ? His dog is named Balrog, but everyone calls him Bal, which could as easily be Baal. The religious theme is reinforced repeatedly, e.g. "Edan" for "Eden", who begins to spontaneously bleed from the palm of one hand. Ananda Caine is doubly significant, linking the Biblical Cain to Ananda, one of Budda's closest disciples. Jared Patterson is the editor of *The Hedgehog* and Jared, which means "descent", is named both as an ancestor of Jesus Christ and a patriarch in the Book of Mormon. Morse's code name during his activist days was Sylvester, and Sylvester was an Anti-Pope during the 11th Century. One of Blair's friends is named Cohen, which is Hebrew for "a priest". The Biblical legend of Armageddon itself includes rumors of Josiah's return from the dead. Other names hint at inhuman forces or the power of the dead, like Gort – who resents being compared to the robot in *The Day The Earth Stood Still*, and Reynard, the trickster from folklore whose legend includes his successful effort to get revenge from beyond the grave. Other names like Lynch and Butcher evoke images of cruel and violent acts.

Blair's disconnection from the world accelerates when he returns to his home. He finds his lover in bed with another man and reads a letter from his agent severing their relationship. His commission to write the article on Lynch's death has been revoked and his partially completed novel seems so pointless that he destroys the manuscript. All of his recent experiences have convinced him that the Nazgul will be return to play "The Armageddon Rag" once more, and the results will be cataclysmic. He retreats into a disreputable apartment where he spends all of his time watching black and white television, particularly re-runs of vintage programs, one last effort to escape into the past.

Then Ananda arrives to tell him that the Nazgul are indeed back together, and that Morse wants him to run their public relations campaign. Blair has misgivings, particularly after attending a less than scintillating rehearsal, but is determined to see things through to their uncertain end. It is not insignificant that the first concert is planned for Chicago, the city where the innocence of the youth movement was crushed by the police riot at the 1968 Democratic Convention, nor that the party is staying at the Bellevue Hotel, namesake of the infamous asylum.

The opening concert is proceeding disastrously, with Richmond clearly incapable of generating the stage presence of the man he was meant to replace, when something very strange happens. He staggers, loses his place for a few seconds, and when he recovers, it is clear that in some manner he has been possessed by the spirit of the original Pat Hobbins. Even his dog recognizes the change. As they continue to recreate the final tour of the original Nazgul, which ended with the assassination outside of Albuquerque, the same bizarre transformation occurs repeatedly, but only when they are playing their old material.

Morse's health begins to deteriorate and it is clear that he is not in control any longer, if he ever was. Blair fears that the final concert will turn into some kind of literal Armageddon, the ultimate battle between good and evil, but wonders "Which side are we?" Answers which seemed self evident when he was younger are now complex and contradictory. When the last concert before Albuquerque devolves into chaos, the authorities move to cancel the next event, and even Edan Morse, now constantly bleeding from invisible wounds, wants to call everything off, fearing that the process he set in motion is now beyond his control.

The author then reveals the truth, that Morse only had the illusion of control. He was manipulated from the outset by Ananda, who was responsible for the murder of Lynch and the firebombing of Gopher John's club. When Morse tries to cancel the concert, she kills him and Gort but spares Blair because the visions have told her that he has a crucial part to play in the final act. Blair, who had become emotionally attached to her, discovers once again that the boundary between good and evil is elusive, if it exists at all, and in his subsequent dream, he has trouble distinguishing between her and the sadistic, fascist Butcher Byrne. It is only then that he decides that he must personally complete the symmetry, that he has to shoot the reincarnated Pat Hobbins during the final concert.

Ambiguity strikes again just as he is preparing to fire and avert Armageddon. Will the death of Hobbins have that result, or will it precipitate it? Blair concludes that the Nazgul were just an instrument, that the purpose of everything that has happened is to make him destroy the thing he once believed in. It is Blair who is bleeding now, his stigmata inflicted during the long climb up a metal tower for the final confrontation. Frustrated, Ananda tries to kill Hobbins herself, but even though her aim is accurate, there is no effect, because things can only advance to the desired conclusion if Blair is the killer.

The Armageddon Rag succeeds in large part because the author recognizes that music does not exist in a vacuum, that it is inextricably linked to its time, and interpreted through the skein of our individual memories. Nor is it an easy matter to distinguish good from evil. The reader isn't likely to sympathize with Dracula's point of view, but it is more difficult to say that Edan Morse or even Ananda Caine was entirely wrong. They perceived themselves as being on the side of good, and one could make a substantial case for that position. It is this complexity which powers the novel, and the lingering questions that make it so memorable.

Ray Cluley's *Probably Monsters*

Ray Cluley is one of the more interesting in the recent crop of new horror writers. His collection, *Probably Monsters* (2015) collected published most of his best short fiction up to that point although a second and smaller collection, *Within the Wind, Beneath the Snow*, also appeared that year. The stories vary considerably in premise and style and are not all horror but several of the authors who have influenced him are specifically cited during the course of the opening story, "All Change," including Ray Bradbury, Arthur Machen, Curt Siodmak, Richard Matheson, and others.

The protagonist is an elderly man who can recognize monsters masquerading as humans and who has a preternatural ability to anticipate where they will appear. He has dispatched many of the creatures over the course of his life and is still active although age has slowed his reflexes. His latest attempt is different, however. He cannot acquire a clear fix on his antagonist, and eventually finds himself on a train all of whose passengers are monsters of one sort or another. He expects to be killed but realizes ultimately that the nature of his secret career has made him into a monster himself, so that he belongs with them. Unless he is imagining the whole thing, which is a distinct possibility.

"I Have Heard the Mermaids Singing" is set in Nicaragua. The protagonist is a rather bitter journalist who has been asked by a friend to write something about the poor medical facilities on the coast, where lobsters are caught by hand and where decompression sickness is a common malady. The local folk legend, still widely believed, is that the men were afflicted by mermaids rather than changes in pressure. It is an interesting story about a man going through a crisis and realizing that life continues even after tragedy, but it is not a horror story despite some ambiguous hints that demons might be real.

"The Festering" has another unhappy protagonist, a teenaged girl living with a mother she hates in a rundown tenement building. She has a desk with a secret drawer, and into the drawer she whispers her secrets, which are generally unpleasant and which involve her opinion of her mother, lies she has told, and similar things. Inside the drawer, a formless gelatinous mass has been created by her worlds, a palpable, visible thing which does not seem to bother her.

Ruby is also having an affair with an adult who lives in the same building and she sometimes makes masks to amuse herself. When the mother discovers the affair, and subsequently unloads a lot of her own secrets while sitting at the desk, the thing in the drawer is apparently overloaded and bursts. Ruby has by this time become an exaggerated version of her mother and the story ends with her whispering secrets into her mother's ear as she lies in a drunken coma. The masks obviously represent the way Ruby and her mother present themselves to the outside world, concealing their own inner natures, and it seems likely that Ruby will repeat her mother's mistakes. The story has a less obvious ending than the first two but does a much better job at evoking an atmosphere of strangeness and vague menace.

"At Night, When the Demons Come" is sent in an apocalyptic Oklahoma in which flying female demons have destroyed most of the world's population. A small group of survivors battles to stay alive in what could almost be a zombie holocaust story. The first hint of the origin of the demons comes quite late: "We made them…when we did what we did to ourselves." We also learn that ordinary women are frequently imprisoned and/or abused because the demons are assumed to be entirely female, although two members of the group have seen a male demon.

The narrator reveals herself to be a woman disguised as a man in order to avoid the obvious bias. She eventually betrays her companions to a group of fanatics because even she has come to believe that women and demons are the same thing. Although this is clearly a commentary on the way women are treated in our society, blamed for all the evils in the world since the Garden of Eden, there is no real explanation of the process in the human mind that gives rise to the prejudice, even though we are seeing everything through the eyes of a woman who has become a believer.

There is a touch of surrealism in "Night Fishing." A young gay man who works as a fisherman and who sometimes encounters the bodies of people who have jumped off the Golden Gate Bridge finds their ghosts appearing on his boat at night. He copies the suicide notes before turning them in as a kind of counterbalance to the fact that his lover – who also committed suicide – never left a proper note of explanation. This was a very poignant character study, not really horror because there is never any real sense of dread or suspense, and it really doesn't work well as a story. The protagonist learns nothing from his encounters with the dead and the closing paragraphs suggest that he never will learn those things he seeks to know.

There is yet another troubled protagonist in "Knock Knock." He is a young boy living with his mother after she has left the boy's criminally abusive father. He dreams that his father returns in the night and knocks on the bedroom door, initially believing that his father is dead because his mother never fully explains the situation. The story is effectively creepy even though most of what happens turns out to be just the boy's imagination. "The Death Drive of Rita, Nee Carina" features a woman badly scarred in an automobile accident that took the lives of her husband and children. She has emerged from the hospital with the conviction that she was spared by a kind of god of road accidents and that she has been called upon to provide fresh sacrifices. To that end she indulges in a series of artifices to cause accidents, most of which involve at least one fatality. The story is a very sharp look into a particularly self destructive insanity.

"The Man Who Was" involves another gay man, an event planner who is skirting around an affair with a prominent military officer turned politician. In due course he discovers that the general is more prosthetic than organic, although the details are more metaphorical than realistic. "Shark! Shark!" is a dark spoof. Some of the people making a shark attack movie turn out to be were-sharks.

"Bloodcloth" is set in a phantasmagorical community where hanging cloths must be fed periodically by the blood of the living, a tribute that no one seems to challenge. When a young girl's father is injured in a mining accident and may be unable to work, it causes a crisis in the family because the mother is currently bedridden as well. The grandmother sacrifices her life to pay the tribute. This is pretty obviously a commentary on taxation and other obligations of society which are often applied disproportionately and without regard to the specific circumstances of the individual.

"The Tilt" follows a man and a woman, both gay but only friends, as they play tourist at a castle somewhere in France. Shortly after arriving the man – whom his friend accuses of being too preoccupied with his sexual orientation – begins to have dreams set in the castle in the past when homosexuals were routinely tortured to death. His uncertainty about his own sexuality has become self destructive and eventually leads to his metaphorical death. "Bones of Crow" is another extended metaphor. A woman who has spent most of her adult life caring for her invalid father sneaks up to the roof of their apartment building to smoke. One day she finds the nest of a giant crow and eventually kills the young birds that emerge from the eggs, but the mother comes back and somehow plucks new young from inside her body. Her final reaction is "joy" as she has finally been released from a life she finds intolerable.

There is still another disturbed personality in "Pins and Needles." James amuses himself by compulsively placing needles and pins in inconspicuous places where random people will stab themselves, the only way he can feel as though he is evoking an emotional response in others after being abandoned by both parents. When he meets a young woman who is clearly attracted to him, the contrary tension confuses him. There's a rather grotesque ending which jars a bit since it doesn't really deal with the interpersonal problems that are the core of the story.

"Gator Moon" is a minor story about a man who accidentally hits another with his car, then clubs him to death when he realizes the man has probably suffered major brain damage. He feels at least marginal guilt and tries to do an anonymous favor for the man's family, but they believe in the power of magic, suspect his involvement, and exact their revenge. In "Where the Salmon Run" a woman is dispatched to a remote part of Russia to help formulate plans to deal with poachers who threaten to deplete the salmon population to dangerously low levels. A melodramatic confrontation follows, but this is not a horror story.

"Indian Giver" is a less impressive story about a tragedy on the fringes of the Old West. "A Mother's Blood" is a very emotional vignette about a mother's dread of her own child. "Travellers' Stay" is a moody piece set in a rundown motel. "No More West" is a vignette about a man who feels compelled to keep moving west. "Beachcoming" describes a brief encounter between a strange boy and an even stranger man on a beach. These are all relatively minor.

Cluley makes use of numerous themes and his settings are particularly varied. His protagonists tend to have severe mental or emotional problems, sometimes accompanied by physical impairments. They often feel as though their lives are out of control, and they are usually right. He rarely employs a decisive ending that ties up the loose ends but rather prefers to suggest possible outcomes, and sometimes does not even go that far, although these last are not generally among his stronger stories. His prose is of very high quality and his characterizations are deft and nuanced. He avoids the familiar tropes of horror fiction and his work bears a slight resemblance to that of Robert Aickman but he seems to be carving out his own individual territory. The potential displayed in this collection is striking.

Horror Stories and Other Horror Stories by Robert Boyczuk

Robert Boyczuk is a writer whose work often fails to fit into easy categories. The opening story of his collection *Horror Stories and Other Horror Stories* (2008) is one of several that are not really horror stories at all. "Query" is an epistolary story consisting of letters from an editor at a publishing house to a prospective writer whose manuscript has been lost due to some unspecified natural disaster that caused part of the building to collapse into a deep chasm. Tantalized by the few pages that survive, the editor organizes an expedition to descend into the chasm and recover the rest of the manuscript, but after shocks and other tribulations eventually wipe out the expedition. The final installment is from his replacement and is a canned rejection letter. It is an obvious satire on the editorial process and the seemingly random nature of acceptance and rejection. Although it is clever and funny it is also not horror.

"Gaytown" is, however, quite creepy. Two gay men, one of whom has not come out to his family, are quarreling as they travel across country. The one who has made his gender choices public is chastising the other for not even providing an introduction to his family. They stop for gas at a dilapidated gas station and, after seeing what appears to be an oversized naked human through a window, they are told by an attendant that they have a leak in their gas tank. The repairs will take at least a day so they are directed to a nearby hotel.

After a couple of hours they realize that they have seen many men but no women since arriving, not even in the bar or restaurant. Nor does the name of the town appear on their road map. The entire community turns out to be gay, but no one talks about it and when one of the newcomers makes a public declaration, he is badly beaten and then abducted by something that is clearly not human. The story is obviously a commentary on the pressures on hidden gays and the reasons why they conceal their feelings, and it appears to be saying that this reticence warps them and turns them into monsters, although the ending is not entirely clear.

"Home" is science fiction with dark overtones. Aboard a starship whose crew are wakened from cryosleep in shifts, one of the maintenance workers is driven insane by the guilt he feels over the accidental death of his brother when they were children. "Assassination and the New World Order" is a parable in which corrupt politicians are murdered for their crimes. "When Fat Men Love Thin Women" is a vignette with no real plot in which a man eats compulsively in response to his affection for a woman.

"Jazz Threnody" is a kind of ghost story, although it is not a human ghost. The protagonist's life has been disintegrating around him when he hears a jazz band play a bit of music that gives him new hope. When he confronts them, they deny having played anything out of the ordinary. He next hears the music from a young man playing on a street corner who also denies having played anything out of the ordinary. The original band is nowhere to be found and the young man is seriously injured when he is struck by a car so both sources of the haunting music are closed to him. What he is actually hearing is the potential, or in some cases lost potential, of the various musicians. His last experience with the music leads to his own effort to regain his long lost affinity for making music, but he realizes that while he may have retained the skills, he has lost the gift.

"Doing Time" is a kind of vampire story. The protagonist steals small bits of lifespan from people with whom he has sex. He has a girlfriend from whom he never takes anything, but unbeknownst to him, her nature resembles his. She finds him with another woman and takes control of the draining process so that she receives its benefits and the other woman dies. The protagonist is found with her dead body and a stash of drugs and is telling the story from his prison cell. A man plummeting to his death after jumping from a building in "Falling" finds that time slows so much that he can indulge in a detailed reconsideration of all of the events which led to his committing suicide.

"Object of Desire" is both science fiction and horror. A spaceship arrives in a charted but uninhabited solar system where it detects a new planet that should not have been there along with other strange data readings. There is significant sexual tension among the crew and after it erupts into a violent argument and nearly a physical confrontation, one of the parties to the tension suddenly disappears from the ship as though he had vanished into thin air. Almost simultaneously a radio beacon is detected on the planet, which is Earthlike. A landing is made during which new and unsuspected sexual tension arises and another crew member disappears. It appears that some force has caused everyone aboard the ship – even the artificial intelligence that serves as captain – to become sexually obsessed with the protagonist. The instrument of this change is alien, perhaps the planet itself, and it will not be happy until she feels the same attraction. Since that is clearly impossible, the story ends with her stranded on the world, doomed by a distorted version of love.

"Shika" is a kind of zombie story set during a future war. Although there is speculation about some kind of biological weapon, no one knows why some people turn into walkers, brain dead but animate. The walkers move about restlessly, as though driven by some inner motive, but they appear to have no real goal. They do not attack the living, but orders are that they are to be shot on sight to keep their numbers down. The protagonist sees one of his comrades suddenly change, but he refrains from killing him despite the clear orders to do so.

As tensions, including sexual ones, proliferate within the unit, the protagonist and the title character discuss the possibility that their superiors know something they have hidden from the troops, that their unit is supposed to be immune to becoming walkers, but is actually vulnerable. And when the second of their number succumbs, it looks like the higher echelons are beginning to panic. When Shika is killed in combat, the protagonist feels a compulsion to walk that has nothing to do with the walkers, signifying that is aversion to the horrors of war that is the cause of the condition.

"Tabula Rasa" involves a game organized by a man who invites all of his male ex-lovers to participate. The game is like a reality show in that they periodically vote to throw someone out, who must therefore make his way from their remote cabin to civilization on his own. The game is his way of symbolically freeing himself from past encumbrances, an observation he freely admits to himself. He has a handgun with which he is prepared to enforce the rules of the game, even though there is a possibility that those expelled might die before finding help. The game is in fact rigged, the protagonist's way of discarding the elements from his past that he finds distasteful. The last guest to survive is allowed to stay and is embraced as a lover, but he knows that it is only a matter of time until he too is cast adrift.

In "The Back Shed" a sculptor feeling ambivalent about his marriage encounters an alien that looks like a human woman and makes love to her, then conceals her in the shed behind his house. He periodically has sex with her in the days that follow, but she neither eats nor sleeps nor speaks. His wife leaves him when his latest work begins to consist of grotesque parodies of her body, apparently expressing some hidden loathing. Eventually he realizes that this is the early stage of a kind of invasion in which people will have their feelings for one another perverted.

"The Uncertainty Principle" is science fiction. A shuttle in the outer solar system suffers a crippling meteorite strike. The three people aboard, including a couple who have recently broken off their relationship, struggle to find a way of surviving the disaster. Monster" is a vignette about Frankenstein's monster living in the Arctic. "The Death Artist" is another vignette about an entertainer who dies at each performance.

"The Love Clinic" is a slightly confusing story about a man who is sexually dysfunctional and who consults a clinic that is supposed to deal with that kind of problem, with unexpected results. "Pirates" is an anachronistic story about a pirate who dreams of the future and keeps videotapes in his cabin. He is further outraged by evidence that some other pirate is butchering everyone aboard each ship encountered.

"Cure for Cancer" features a man who becomes infatuated with the woman sent to audit his tax returns. He is a scientist who knows how to induce cancers in people and when his lover threatens to break things off, he considers giving her cancer so that he can save her and thus win back her affections. His miracle cure turns out to be the agency by which the cancer causes her to mutate into something other than human.

The title story involves a police officer who is part of a team investigating a series of mutilation murders. He believes that he has seen the killer, a woman, coalescing out of the shadows themselves. His final confrontation with the killer is not remotely what he had expected it to be.

Most of these are stories of the weird but not really horror. Only a few develop any suspense or sense of terror, and that is by design.

The author shows us distorted versions of the real world, and by distorting them, points out idiosyncrasies that might otherwise have escaped our attention.

Susie Moloney's Things Withered

Susie Moloney is the author of a handful of suspense novels and a slightly larger handful of short stories. Her collection, *Things Withered* (2013) maintains a very high quality throughout and I suspect that if there were more widely distributed publications featuring horror fiction, she would be considerably better known than she is. Several of the stories are more weird than horrific but there is a fairly consistent tone that the world is a dangerous place and that we are all prey for threats that arise both internally and externally.

The opening story, "The Windemere", is a case in point. Moloney established the character of Anita, the protagonist, carefully and with considerable depth. Anita works in a real estate office where she has been overlooked for promotion for many years. In her fifties now, she has an ongoing struggle to control her weight and she is aware that her appearance is one of the major problems she faces in dealing with her authoritarian and arbitrary boss. The Windemere is a condominium in her territory and she has recently sold the unit of an elderly woman who inexplicably fell to her death from the window to a younger woman, Stephanie.

A few weeks later another resident has a fatal heart attack, and a friend named Stephanie introduces one of her acquaintances who is interested in the suddenly vacant apartment. A third death – followed by another woman introduced by Stephanie - begins to feel like too much of a coincidence, but Anita needs the commission to keep her boss off her back. Nevertheless, she realizes that not only will she never be promoted, but that things are being arranged so that her performance will drop, presumably as the first step in a campaign to replace her with a younger woman.

When she realizes that she detected salt spilled in all three apartments where the deaths occurred, and then hears the three women chanting one night, she concludes that they are witches, although the author never uses that word. The death of an older couple who are also residents frees up another unit, but when Stephanie introduces yet another prospective tenant, Anita tells her that the vacancy is already spoken for by her very own boss. He dies a few days later in an automobile accident and the rest is left to the reader's imagination. The story is very well constructed, packing a good deal of both plot and characterization into a relatively short space.

There is a similarly unsuccessful protagonist in "The Truckdriver," but he is much younger, barely out of school. Although he has yet to find a job that pays a decent wage, he becomes obsessed with an antique truck that has been painted lime green and buys it from its owner. There is a suggestion buried within the transaction that there is something unusual about the truck, but the young man seems oblivious to the undertones. The obsession comes to dominate his life and ultimately drives him to commit a horrible act.

The protagonist of "Wife" is so conditioned to performing household duties in a prescribed fashion that she feels guilty when she varies her routine. She is obsessed with the need to act "normal" and bored with her existence. At times she feels deep guilt about unspecified acts in her past. She and her husband have no children and it is unclear whether or not this is voluntary. The internal contradictions finally push her toward behavior she thought confined to her past, smoking, picking up men in bars. But she has changed and the boredom and frustration have evolved into rage, which explodes during sex with a stranger.

"Poor David, or, the Possibilities of Coincidence in Situations of Multiple Occurrences" is a very strange story centered on a young couple. Neither Myra nor David have fully made the transition from adolescent to adult and they have deferred marriage, although Myra is maturing rapidly. David has always been dominated by his overly attentive mother and has a somewhat fragile personality. So when he finds his wife's aunt dead of a heart attack, it affects him deeply, and this is reinforced a few weeks later when he decides to ask his boss for a raise and discovers that he has just hanged himself in his office. He and Myra decide to get married but pressure about the wedding, his mother's insistence that he go back to school, and his dread of finding another body begin to push David toward collapse. A third dead body leaves him even less tethered to reality, but ultimately Myra pulls him through. Not technically horror, although David's feeling that he has become the specter of death is suitably creepy.

"The Last Living Summer" is about a handful of people surviving on a beach after some unspecific apocalypse. This is more of a portrait of a situation than a story. In "The Audit" another mildly dysfunctional couple are facing an audit of the female partner's wages, and she has never declared her tips as income even though she works as a waitress. As she prepares for the audit, the paperwork with which she has never felt easily seems to be multiplying of its own accord and her accountant keeps calling to ask for things she doesn't even comprehend. While the idea of a tax audit may indeed be horrible, there is no actually menace although the woman is finally killed by an apparent plethora of paper cuts. The protagonist, however, is another of the author's characters who does not seem capable of understanding the world and is caught up by forces beyond his understanding.

In "Petty Zoo" a children's zoo at a mall turns into a nightmare when the animals begin attacking the visitors. This is a good example of Moloney's ability to turn the most innocuous things into bizarre and terrifying alternatives. "Night Beach" concerns a young woman whose affair with a married man has just ended badly. She has rented a beach house in a remote town, but is puzzled by the fact that she never sees anyone else on the beach, even though it is in a tourist area, and by the town itself, which seems strangely indolent. Before leaving on her vacation, she had mailed detailed proof to her ex-lover's wife that he had been unfaithful. A local person tells her the beach is popular only at night, so she returns that evening and finds a number of people there, although some of them do not seem to be completely aware of their surroundings. It becomes increasingly obvious that they are all dead, and then the real townspeople show up and drown her, an annual sacrifice that brings life to their community, not an original concept but handled in a nicely twisted manner.

A woman is sent off to rehab in "The Human Society" and her equally alcoholic boyfriend is supposed to look after her two dogs while she is gone. He dumps them at the humane society, in large part because his brain is so fried that he fails to understand what he is doing. This is another piece that is more portrait than story. "Reclamation on the Forest Floor" opens with the college student protagonist standing over the body of the woman she has just bludgeoned to death and dragged into the woods. She returns to college but some of the physical changes that presumably are occurring to the corpse are bothering her as well. Her arm itches and when it is wiped, the residue is green, and she seems to smell badly despite showering, and attracts large numbers of flies. She also finds twigs and dirt in her apartment and while some of this might be hallucinatory, some of it is visible to other people. In fact the dead woman is being restored to life as her killer undergoes all of the elements of putrefaction. This is a very creepy story.

"Domestic Happiness" is an enigmatic vignette about a woman who sacrifices two fingers in return for help keeping her life in order. "I (heart) Dogs" is about a woman dealing with her elderly, sickly aunt and a dying dog, pestered by a thoughtless neighbor who is eventually attacked by one of the dogs. This also is a portrait rather than a story.

"The Neighbourhood, or, to the Devil With You" features another older protagonist, this one dealing with the fact that she hates the woman across the street, a nasty, bullying busybody. She reflects upon an accident years earlier when one of the children in the neighborhood was beheaded in an almost impossible accident that Hazel, the obnoxious neighbor, had inadvertently precipitated. The death of a neighbor's dog, the body found in her yard, and another fatal accident next door establish Hazel as a witch in the eyes of the local children and she withdraws even further from the community around her. Finally Hazel tells the narrator that the new man next door never sleeps, that he has a tail, and that she has seen him eating grass. The obvious conclusion is that she has become senile. But in fact the neighbor turns out to be the devil, to whom Hazel at some point sold her soul.

Moloney's horrors are generally quiet ones, and more often than not the horrors that are inflicted upon her characters are inflicted in large part by the characters themselves.

The Schweitzer Mythos

The Cthulhu Mythos created by H.P. Lovecraft has inspired a great many writers to add to that world, either through pastiches that try to emulate the narrative style if not the somewhat artificial prose of the originals through innovative tales that explore new possibilities and permutations. Darrell Schweitzer who among his various accomplishments has served as editor of Weird Tales is one of these writers. His Lovecraftian stories take place in various historical periods and, unlike most of those who have written Mythos pastiches, he frequently employs children as protagonists.

Awaiting Strange Gods (Fedogan & Bremer, 2015) collected several of Schweitzer's Lovecraftian tales and some other weird fiction in a single volume. The collection opens with "Envy, the Garden of Ynath, and the Sin of Cain." A lonely college student who has always had trouble finding a place in life takes as his mentor a mysterious figure who paints landscapes from other worlds and who possesses an arcane talent for initiating mental voyages among the planes of reality.

The younger man, Brian Simmons, is ambivalent about the relationship and even compares his mentor to Satan. They have an encounter with otherworldly forces in the forest and the mentor is taken to Ynath. Simmons feels abandoned and turns toward normality, but more than two decades later his friend returns, briefly founds a cult which is soon dispersed, and then the two reunite, their relationship radically altered, and it is Simmons who figures out what the alien intelligences desire. The plot is not complex and is really subordinate to the evocation of a atmosphere of weirdness and wonderment.

"Hanged Man and Ghost" involves a school teacher introduced into a small, remote Pennsylvania community, unaware of the fact that the inhabitants have unusual powers and dark secrets. This might have been a very minor story but it is enhanced by an intriguing underlying mythology and its narration by a well realized young boy. "Sometimes You Have to Shout About It" is more of a character study, a troubled young girl whose parents, and later a kind of stepfather, are engaged in arcane worship while she herself has the ability to shout loud enough to penetrate into another world.

In "Stragglers from Carrrhae" two Roman soldiers fleeing a battlefield defeat encounter a corpse reanimated by Nyarlathotep which begins following them. The author adopts a mildly bantering tone in this one that is quite entertaining, but the story itself has a relatively weak conclusion. "The Eater of Hours" also has an historical setting, the Crusades. A group of fugitive crusaders take refuge in a strange tower where time and identity are not always certain. "The Runners Beyond the Wall" is set in a less clearly defined past. A young boy, the sole survivor of a shipwreck, is given refuge on the estate of an unusual aristocrat who appears to have drawn the boy toward him. The Lovecraftian references in this one are relatively minor.

"On the Eastbound Train" takes place on the Orient Express. Two scholars are traveling together when one, the protagonist, realizes that his companion has become involved with something mysterious and dangerous. He is unable to elicit any details and then one night their cabin is invaded by hooded men who knock him unconscious and carry off his colleague. Illusions and the protagonist's own lies cloud the conclusion but it appears that he has willingly joined the cult which kidnapped the other professor and the two of them have both been willingly working on their nefarious researches ever since.

A young boy enjoys an affinity with darkness in "Howling in the Dark" and senses that there are living beings concealed within it. This is primarily another character study with a minimal plot. "The Head Shop in Arkham", original to this collection, is a less than entirely serious story. The owner of a comic book and hippie related paraphernalia shop calls himself Nigel, but his real name is Nyarlathotep.

"Innsmouth Idyll" tells the story of a boy discovering his true nature when his parents die and he moves to Innsmouth, there to discover that he is not entirely human. An older man reunited with people he knew as children begins to remember the very odd things that they were taught in school in "Class Reunion." The vignette, "Why We Do It," is a loose sequel to "Hanged Man and Ghost." A college student from that same odd town lures a classmate back so that she can be sacrificed to a bloodthirsty god.

An artist and a ghoul strike up a brief, quasi-friendship in "Warm." The protagonist of "Spiderwebs in the Dark" runs a book shop and has an unusual customer who seems to travel all over the world and who has impossible knowledge of the past of everyone whom he meets. He is shown that time and space are all interrelated, and that a terrible menace hovers over them all.

The spirit of a dead man is summoned to solve a murder in "The Corpse Detective" In "Jimmy Bunny" a housebreaker visits a supposedly untenanted home and finds references to his own childhood in one of the rooms. Unfortunately they include the return of his abusive father. "The Last of the Black Wine" is more reminiscent of Clark Ashton Smith than of Lovecraft. A poet living at the end of the Earth when all of its gods and goddesses have died has an encounter with sorcery. An adventurer meets his doom in the somewhat similar "In Old Commorium."

"The Clockwork King, the Queen of Glass, and the Man with the Hundred Knives" is in some ways a rewrite of "Envy, the Garden of Ynath, and the Sin of Cain." The protagonist has a brilliant but possibly unbalanced college friend who disappears for many years, then reappears with stories of a fault in the border between realities. "Ghost Dancing" takes place shortly after a gigantic tentacled monster rises from the ocean to destroy much of Manhattan. Similar disasters occur all over the world as the reign of humanity over the Earth is abruptly brought to an end by the return of the Old Ones.

Two of the stories are collaborations with Jason Hollander. "The Scroll of the Worm" concerns a woman who attends a party hoping to make connections to advance her career, but who instead encounters a raving man who warns her about the dangers of a forbidden scroll, with disastrous consequences. A man returns to his home town in "Those of the Air" to discover the existence of mysterious and deadly beings and have his life changed irrevocably.

Although Schweitzer draws on the traditions and even some of the tropes of classic writers of weird fiction, he has a distinctive touch of his own, often involving dreams and hallucinations. At his best, he creates genuinely disturbing landscapes across which his characters move, often to their doom. Even at his weakest, he is invariably entertaining.

Rick Yancey's Monster Hunters

Although Rick Yancey's novels have been marketed for young adults, they are written in a style that also appeals to more sophisticated readers. His newest series opened with *The Fifth Wave*, which as of this writing has just been released as a major motion picture. His previous series about Will Henry, apprentice to a monster hunter, consists of four volumes of which *The Monstrumologist* (2009) was the first. They are set in America during the Victorian era and Henry is a twelve year old boy who in 1888 goes to live with an eccentric scholar – Dr. Pellinore Warthrop - whose investigations are often frowned upon by the authorities. Henry's parents died in a fire and there was nowhere else for him to go. He is the narrator, although the story is contained in journals he wrote as an adult and not long before his own death.

In the opening volume, a grave robber brings a mysterious bundle to Warthrop one evening. It contains the partially eaten corpse of a young girl and the eater, a headless male humanoid whom Warthrop calls an anthropophagus. These are humanoid creatures with their mouths in their bellies and they are essentially ghouls. The puzzling thing in this case is that the creature – which is native to Africa but not the Americas - has itself died, although there is initially no apparent cause of death. Warthrop performs an autopsy and discovers that it choked to death on a necklace it swallowed. It also implanted an infant of its own race in the girl's body, which Warthrop extracts and kills. This sequence is unusually intense and graphic for a book aimed at younger readers.

Warthrop explains to Henry that this type of creature is immensely strong, can leap as far as forty feet in a single bound, and generally hunts in packs. They prefer live prey but obviously also eat the dead. He concludes that there must be at least two more of the creatures at large, both females, but cannot imagine how they reached North America. Nor does he understand how the anthropophagus could have been inside the coffin while there was no sign that the ground above had been disturbed.

Accompanied by the grave robber, they visit the cemetery but are unable to detect any intruders until the ground erupts beneath their companion, who is dragged down screaming until Warthrop kills him with a revolver. The two of them barely escape with their lives when they are attacked by a horde of the creatures rather than just a pair, and they only do so by throwing them the corpse of the young girl they had planned to re-inter.

Warthrop and Henry visit an asylum where they interview the sea captain who once worked for Warthrop's father and who confesses that he traveled to Benin where he purchased three of the anthropophagi and conveyed them back to New England per instructions. Conditions at the asylum are horrific – the captain dies of neglect within hours of their interview – and Warthrop vows that the administrators will be sent to jail. Henry overhears some local gossip that involves Warthrop's father, who pursued similar investigations, and who was known to have consulted with two Confederate agents during the Civil War, which results in a heated argument between him and Warthrop, who later suggests that perhaps his father intended to attempt to breed a less malevolent strain of anthropophagi and sought funding or support wherever he could find it.

The local constable arrives with news of a terrible tragedy for which he desires Warthrop's expertise. The local minister, his wife, and all but one of his young children have been slaughtered by parties unknown in their church. Some of the bodies show signs of having been partially devoured. Henry had tried to get Warthrop to warn the local people about the creatures in the cemetery but had been told that the pack would not be hungry again for at least three days, a prediction that is now quite evidently wrong. Henry blames his mentor silently for the death of the family.

Shortly thereafter the constable discovers that Warthrop already knew of the existence of the creatures. He threatens to arrest him and the surviving son of the butchered family, Malachi, assaults him before Henry is able to calm him down. Then John Kearns arrives, an associate whom Warthrop had written to about the matter, and the reader is warned that while Warthrop only hunts monsters to study them and reduce their menace, Kearns hunts them for amusement and is a monster of sorts himself.

Kearns has experience with the anthropophagi and agrees to exterminate them contingent on a fee – which Warthrop agrees to pay – and immunity from prosecution for any laws he might break in the process. He also asserts that the most likely explanation for their presence is that Warthrop's father bred them and fed them until his death five years earlier, following which they escaped from wherever they had been confined and have been living on corpses until quite recently. Kearns has a much simpler philosophy than Warthrop: "There is no morality except the morality of the moment." He organizes a group of men into a hunting party and allows, in fact encourages Malachi to accompany them.

Kearns also indicates that humans and the monsters have a lot in common "the only significant difference being that they have yet to master our expertise in hypocrisy, the gift of our superior intellect that enables us to slaughter one another in droves, more often than not under the auspices of an approving god." Although Warthrop expresses disgust, Kearns has made a point.

Kearns baits his trap with what appears to be a fresh corpse, but in fact the woman is alive and begins to struggle when he cuts her open to provide the smell of blood. When the first creature appears, Kearns cripples but does not kill it with gunfire in order to lure out the others. Warthrop and Henry rescue the woman and carry her to comparative safety.

Although the ambush is successful and results in a mass slaughter of the creatures, the matriarch of the group is not present and there may be other survivors. The only solution is to pursue them in their warrens beneath the cemetery. The entrance to the warren is a secret passage through the Warthrop family tomb, confirming at least part of Kearns' theory that the creatures were raised in captivity. A charnel house filled with human bones proves they were interred there for twenty years, but it is not clear whether or not their food was provided to them living or already dead. Kearns, Warthrop, and Malachi descend into the tomb unaccompanied initially, but after a few minutes Warthrop insists that Henry must join them. He does so, and sees evidence that the victims were in fact alive when they were given to the anthropophagi.

He is the only one small enough to investigate the only tunnel out of the first chamber. He reaches the opposite end, but falls out and down an unclimbable slope, trapping himself in the space where the creatures have built their nests. He manages to kill a young anthropophagus but is himself wounded in the process. Lost, he eventually encounters Kearns, who tricks him into acting as bait for the rest of the creatures. He is rescued by the rest of the party, which separates again and in the final confrontation Malachi is killed by the last of the anthropophagi, who in turned is killed by Henry.

There is a brief follow up in which the details of the preservation of the anthropophagi – the doctor in charge of the sanitarium was sending patients to be eaten – and Kearns kills both of the men who were involved. Warthrop's father apparently believed he could tame them and that on balance his work would be beneficial, but he was wrong on both counts. Kearns disappears and there is a suggestion that he may also be Jack the Ripper. Henry also learns that he has been infected by a benevolent organism that will extend his life far beyond its usual length.

Yancey presents a rather nuanced Warthrop, whom his protagonist credits as possessing "overweening ambition and pride" and who puts a young boy into dangerous situations without the slightest hesitation. Henry has other reservations about his mentor. Warthrop asserts that fear is the only enemy, but Henry believes that there are times when fear is important to survival. "I, at twelve, had only the inarticulate protests of a child whose acute sense of justice has been offended by the pious rationalizations of an authoritarian adult." Warthrop has "not the slightest shred of humility or warmth." On the other hand, Warthrop has a strong sense of justice and when pushed to extremities, displays his affection for Henry, though in rather unorthodox ways. Henry himself muses that the human curse "is to never really know one another." And even when Henry is himself an elderly man, he asserts that he does not understand the bonds between them but that he knows that he never loved Warthrop.

Kearns enlarges on his philosophy toward the end. The human race, he announces, is doomed because "it has fallen in love with the pleasant fiction that we are somehow above the rules that we have determined rule everything else." For all of his repulsive acts, Kearns is not an entirely unadmirable figure. He, like all of the other characters, is more deeply drawn than is usual in young adult fiction, or most adult genre fiction for that matter.

Will Henry's second memoir was *The Curse of the Wendigo* (2010). Warthrop has been chosen to rebut a member of the Monstrumologists' society who proposes adding various supernatural creatures to the list of cryptids they are investigating, which arouses the wrath of those members who believe that they are scientists and not occultists. He is in the midst of preparing his response when Mrs. Muriel Chanler shows up at his house. She has received a letter from Pierre Larose who was acting as guide for her husband John, whom he suggests has been carried off by a wendigo. Henry detects that there is unusual tension between Chanler and his mentor, but no one explains its nature to him, although it appears to be that she rejected him romantically for John Chanler. Warthrop refuses to accept the possibility that a wendigo exists and given that John has been missing for three months, he sees no reason to assume that he is still alive.

After she leaves - disappointed by his insensitivity - he has second thoughts and sets out with Henry to Canada by train to investigate. They are unable to find Larose, who has dropped out of sight, but they do hear of a shaman named Jack Fiddler whom Larose had mentioned in his letter to Muriel. They receive the assistance of a Northwest Mounted Policeman named Jonathan Hawk, who offers to guide them to Fiddler's encampment.

En route, they find Larose dead, impaled on a broken tree, the skin flayed from his body. When they reach the village, Fiddler is evasive and early the following morning Warthrop finds Chanler – comatose and wasted – and organizes a rescue despite the active opposition of the tribesmen, who believe that Chanler belongs to the Wendigo and must be treated ritually.

Their trek back toward civilization is tortuous. They sense that something is following or watching them. Chanler is no better and their food has run out. Hawk begins to act irrationally and poses another potential danger. Then one night he disappears and Warthrop and Henry are left alone with the unconscious man. They struggle on and eventually find the body of their erstwhile guide, frozen solid near the top of a tree. When Henry climbs up to help recover the body, he sees a town in the distance but before they reach it, Chanler attacks him and some mysterious force rips their tent apart and follows them, although Warthrop – determined not to believe in the supernatural – attempts to rationalize events after the fact.

Henry is unconscious for three days and when he recovers, Chanler appears to be much better, though still thin. There is, however, tension between him and Warthrop that Henry doesn't understand, and there is foreshadowing that this is not the same John Chanler who set out on the expedition. Muriel retrieves him and takes him back to New York to complete his recovery.

Warthrop – whose stiff and sometimes unintentionally cruel attitude was established in the first book – softens slightly in this one and we learn more about the vicissitudes of his youth. He offers Henry the choice of moving to another home, which is tearfully declined, after which the two travel to New York themselves to present the refutation of Dr. Helrung's newest paper. There they meet various other delegates and are invited to dine with Helrung at his home, where they meet his niece, Lillian Bates, who is Henry's age. They also run into Muriel Chanler, who confesses that her husband seems to have developed a new and rather crude cast to his personality following his ordeal.

Chanler is being kept in Helrung's house where he refuses to eat because he cannot name the food he desires – which is of course human flesh. Warthrop insists that he suffers from derangement and malnutrition and demands that he be taken to a hospital for treatment while Helrung insists that they can do nothing for him because his ailment is spiritual and supernatural. Muriel confesses to Warthrop that she has lost hope for her husband's recovery and admits that she has loved Warthrop since they first met, despite her marriage to his friend.

Chanler disappears from the hospital – apparently through a fourth floor window – after killing the man who was watching over him and stealing the heart from the corpse. Helrun asserts that he has become a wendigo, but Warthrop still insists that there has to be a rational explanation. That seems even more unlikely when John Chanler kills three more people in brutal fashion and carries off his wife. She is found dead later and Warthrop is arrested. Will is badly mistreated by the police who want him to testify that he witnessed the murder.

Although Warthrop and Henry are released, both are injured. Helrung – who is obviously the prototype for Van Helsing since he is a friend of Bram Stoker – employs a doctor named Seward, confirming the reference – organizes a hunt. (Algernon Blackwood also has a cameo appearance as a reporter.) A group of monstrumologists forms and, with Henry accompanying them, they set off for the slum district to investigate three mysterious deaths or disappearances the previous night. They form three teams and Henry accompanies two strangers, one of whom is promptly killed when they investigate a recently abandoned building. Henry is taken captive, but Warthrop shows up in time to engage Chanler in battle, during which Henry kills him with a silver knife. Even then, Warthrop refuses to believe that he really was a wendigo and he is broken hearted when the society votes to include supernatural entities in its purview henceforth.

The second book was considerably different from the first, with multiple locations, more adventurous situations, and considerably more depth to both of the main characters. It is even more explicitly horrifying, with faces ripped from skulls, dead babies, impalements, and so forth but the intensity of those sequences is well suited to the tone of the story. Both Henry and Warthrop are at the end convinced that they have made bad choices and that they should have known better.

The Isle of Blood (2011) is the longest in the series. John Kearns has sent a package to Warthrop, ensuring its delivery by pretending to have poisoned the messenger and telling him that only Warthrop can provide the antidote, for which Warthrop supplies a mild mixture or morphine to calm the man's nerves. The package contains a mysterious kind of nest which Warthrop forbids Henry to touch. The messenger, Wymond Kendall, did touch it and in due course he begins to decay and turns into a mindless killer whom Warthrop is forced to dispatch with a revolver. Since Henry was physically attacked, he is subjected to a painful decontamination process which includes the amputation of one finger.

They promptly set off for New York where they confer with Professor Helrung. The nest is a rarity, but the creature that makes it – the magnificum – is the rarest of all, for no one is known to have ever actually seen one. Warthrop is determined that he shall be the first, by tracking down the source of the nest. He also believes that Kearns is seeking the same thing, for reasons of his own. In New York they are introduced to Thomas Arkwright, an apprentice monstrumologist who seems to know a great deal about Warthrop and his recent activities. Henry instinctively mistrusts him and is certain that he is lying about having written to Warthrop numerous times since Henry himself sorts the correspondence.

One morning Henry discovers that Warthrop has gone off to Europe with Arkwright without him and he is put into the care of the Bates family – we know he will eventually marry their daughter – who plan to adopt him after several months have passed with no word from Warthrop. Henry never stops resenting his desertion and is not happy where he is, and one day he analyzes the situation the way he believes Warthrop would have done and finds contradictions in Arkwright's story. Arkwright, meanwhile, sends a telegram indicating that Warthrop is dead and that he is returning to New York.

Henry convinces Van Helrung and another monstrumologist named Jacob Torrance that Arkwright is a fake and he is taken prisoner upon his return. Torrance threatens to infect him with the nest if he does not tell them the truth and he finally admits that he works for British Intelligence, that Warthrop is alive and captive in a remote place, and that there are other forces at work which he refuses to identify. To Henry's horror, Torrance infects Arkwright anyway, insisting that they cannot allow him to report to the authorities about his own kidnapping or alert others whose plans may be inimical to those of Henry and Van Helrung. He locks Arkwright in with a revolver loaded with a single round and the prisoner kills himself.

Henry, Torrance, and Van Helrung then set off to England to try to pick up Warthrop's trail. They are met by a colleague, Hiram Walker. Warthrop was committed to an insane asylum by Arkwright, who is suspected to have been a double agent actually working for the Tsar of Russia. They enlist the aid of Arthur Conan Doyle to secure his release. Although they are successful, when they return to their hotel – shadowed by agents of the Russian secret police – they find Torrance dead, his throat cut.

Warthrop then recounts his earlier adventures. He and Arkwright were captured by two Russian security men but were released because the Russians believed that they were mistaken about where the magnificum nest was found – fooled by a clever lie concocted by Warthrop, who was not killed because the Russians thought it was a great joke to have him institutionalized.

Warthrop and Henry set off alone for Socotra, the island where the nest actually originated, but while in Venice they discover that the two Russians are still following them. They take steps to at least temporarily elude them and travel to Aden, where Warthrop looks up Arthur Rimbaud, the famous poet turned adventurer. In search of transport to Socotra, Warthrop goes off alone and the two Russians show up and accost Henry. Since they do not expect a young boy to be armed, they are taken by surprise when he draws a revolver and kills both of them. He never tells Warthrop what happened because the latter has expressed fear that their association might coarsen the boy.

They come ashore at last despite terrible storms and visit a village that has been wiped out by the rotting disease that follows contact with the nest of the magnificum. They start toward the next town and are interrupted in their journey by a rain of human flesh, another sign of the creature they seek. A short while later they find John Kearns, or he finds them. He eventually explains that the magnificum is the ultimate monster – it is humanity itself, and the disease is just a peculiarly repulsive plague. They also find a baby that appears to be immune and when Henry is infected, they use a sample of its blood to save him. He recovers while they are waiting for the boat to return to pick them up, but it becomes obvious that Kearns is planning to kill them both so Henry – without consulting Warthrop – employs a clever ruse and stabs Kearns to death.

Although *The Isle of Blood* is very similar to the first two in the series, it has some minor pacing problems which were at least partly unavoidable given the nature of the plot. There is very little sense of menace until quite late in the story and the two Russian spies have no depth as characters. There is some development of the relationship between the two main protagonists, but Henry seems relatively unchanged despite the events that have taken place during the course of the three books.

The final volume in the series was *The Final Descent* (2013), which jumps around in time to Henry's first days with Warthrop, to a time after they have parted, and other stops in between. Sixteen year old Will Henry has more self confidence and more than a casual interest in Lillian Bates, despite Warthrop's warning that his extended life expectancy makes romantic entanglements unwise.

The main story involves Henry at sixteen. A mysterious visitor named Maeterlinck arrives promising to supply a living example of an unidentified but very rare creature for a fee of one million dollars. Warthrop throws him out but Henry secretly agrees to meet with him at the local inn, where he drugs the man after seeing that he has in his possession a viable egg from a species believed extinct. Henry has become coarsened by his association with Warthrop and sees this as a way to show that he has grown independent of his mentor and capable of achieving great things on his own.

The story jumps back and forth in time – probably a bit too much – but whatever the creature was, Henry showed it to Warthrop and it is secured in the monstrumology museum in New York until someone murders two people in the process of stealing it. Henry finds the surviving thief, who is dying, and realizes that the creature is now inside the thief's body. Warthrop extracts it and they return it to captivity only to have another burglar make off with it a short time later. The venom of the creature is the most addictive narcotic in the world, hence it is extremely valuable.

Will misunderstands the situation, as a result of which he kills two men who are related to the leader of the Black Hand, an Italian criminal organization, putting in jeopardy both his and Warthrop's lives as well as any chance of recovering the missing creature. Ensuing events put an unbearable strain upon the relations between the two and ultimately they go their separate ways. Henry's bitterness and Warthrop's contradictory feelings make up most of the tension in the story, despite the presence of a fabulous creature and various violent criminals. The reader is shown the end of their collaboration, and its odd if rather brief rekindling many years later.

Yancey writes with a degree of sophistication all too rare in young adult literature. His characters are both flawed and heroic and they meet the challenges they face in very different ways. The series will almost certainly become a staple of YA literature, although the very graphic imagery may render it controversial in some quarters.

Every House Is Haunted by Ian Rogers

The lack of a major, regular magazine for horror fiction is particularly frustrating since much of the best of the genre appears in short form. A case in point is the work of Ian Rogers, a Canadian writer whose short fiction, though uneven, is undeservedly difficult to find. This was his second collection; the first was a series of tales about a detective who investigated the supernatural. The stories are loosely collected into sections referring to parts of a house – the attic, the library, etc.

The collection opens with "Aces", which is not really horror. A young man trying to raise his teenaged sister observes several instances in which things appear or disappear magically, and she insists that she has an invisible companion who is not human. Eventually two official looking people arrive, tell him that his sister is altering the nature of reality, and drive off with her, supposedly to some place secure where she won't destroy the world. The nicely constructed sense of weirdness is rather dissipated by the lack of a resolution. "Autumnology" is a vignette about a tree trapped in perpetual autumn.

"Cabin D" involves a decrepit cabin which kills everyone who tries to spend a night there. Although largely forgotten, it is remembered by a small group of people, one of whom is terminally ill and who decides to expend his life in destroying the cabin's malevolent force forever by means of his psychic powers, which he does. Although well written, the story is oddly disjointed – the first half is about his last meals in a small diner and it has no connection to the second half, which ends with a whimper rather than a bang.

"Winter Hammock" is a post apocalypse story, a disaster more like the one in "The Mist" by Stephen King, with monsters whose very nature is incomprehensible. The protagonist and only character is living in a warehouse surrounded by various weird creatures where he slowly but inevitably goes insane. "A Night in the Library with the Gods" is a non-story. A man with no memories finds himself in a mysterious library room whose books are a kind of access to extradimensional gods, but nothing happens as a result of the revelation, which is not novel enough to make the story successful.

"The Nanny" is another non-story. A psychic woman is sent into a haunted house to communicate with the two dead children haunting it and she decides to read them a story. It ends with her opening the book, but we never learn how the children came to die there or what happens to them after she begins to read. "The Dark and the Young" has a strong narrative though it reads like the opening chapter of a novel. A young woman is recruited into a secret government project to decipher an ancient book that is actually a conduit through which creatures can be drawn from other worlds, although at the cost of human sacrifices. When the project begins sacrificing babies, she and a couple of co-workers rescue a group of potential victims and steal the book so that there will be no way to continue the project, and the story ends with them fleeing, unable to think of a way to destroy the book.

"The Currents" is a fantasy about a man who rides the river currents from place to place. "Leaves Brown" is also a non-story. An old man tells his grandson that the island where they live is home to creatures only visible to a very few, but they don't see any of them and nothing happens. "Wood" is a vignette about sentient trees. "The House on Ashleigh Avenue" is a fairly conventional haunted house story. A secret organization investigating the paranormal has been keeping certain pieces of property off the market for the safety of the public, but one of their members went rogue and sold the house. Although the story is nicely intense, the back story is irritating because it is unresolved and unexplained. Why did the man go rogue when he had nothing to gain and knew that he was putting the new owners in jeopardy? The story could have easily been constructed without this major loose end, so its inclusion is puzzling.

"The Rifts Between Us" has an interesting premise. Scientists discover that people who are dying are able to access rifts in reality and explore a realm between life and death. Unfortunately, something from the world of the dead decides to reverse the process and explore the reality of the living. "Vogo" is a vignette about a creature in a lake that is apparently in fact the ghost of a creature in the lake. "The Cat" is one of the best stories in the collection, short but succinct. A new family cat is such an excellent hunter and family protector that it even kills the neighborhood drug dealer.

"Deleted Scenes" is not horror, but it is quite clever. A minor actor takes a job performing in deleted scenes, scenes that are predetermined will not appear in the final movie, until he is kidnapped by a cult that wants to make all deleted scenes public. "Tattletail" is a mildly funny spoof about a boy with a pet demon in an alternate world where that actually makes sense. "Charlotte's Frequency" is an effective story in which a strange spider turns an entire house into an extension of its web.

In "Relaxed Best" a private detective follows a possibly wayward husband to a strange nightclub that is disconnected from time and reality. "Hunger" is a very short prose poem about some kind of apocalyptic collapse, but there is no plot. "Inheritor" opens with the estranged son of a dead man discovering that the family home where his sister died of a mysterious illness has not been sold after all and that he has inherited it, along with the key of a safety deposit box. Despite his aversion to the house, he visits it and discovers that his sister is not dead but has turned into some kind of monster. The deposit box holds a gun with which he kills her. "Twillingate" is a mild encounter with ghostly figures and the final story, "The Candle," has a man discovering that the world has changed around him in a matter of minutes.

Rogers has an excellent prose style and when married to a strong plot, the results are notably good. There is a tendency to focus on an unusual situation or image and expand upon it without actually introducing a structured narrative, and while some of these enjoy a limited success, many of them seem incomplete, or their endings abruptly truncated. It is possible that Rogers would be more consistently successful at novel length where a more structured plot would be necessary.

Three Novels by Eric Red

Eric Red is an American screenwriter and director, perhaps best known for the movies *Near Dark*, a vampire film, and *The Hitcher*, an indefinable but memorably creepy movie. The quality of those films was promising but his prose work is less appealing. His first novel, *Don't Stand So Close* (2011), was a thriller and his second was supernatural horror.

The Guns of Santa Sangre (2013) is set in the Old West. John Whistler is a bounty hunter pursuing three wanted men in Mexico when his stagecoach breaks down and he is forced to spend a night in the desert with the two coachmen and a young prostitute. They are attacked by a pack of werewolves and wiped out, establishing the tone of the novel.

Next we meet a small time thief named Alvarez who is the only survivor when the pack attacks a small stagecoach station. He is taken into custody by the Mexican police and thrown in a cell, but he has been bitten and it is only a matter of time until he becomes one of the shape changers. Fortunately one of the prisoners recognizes what he is and, improbably, the jailers never searched and found his derringer and providential silver bullets, so he kills the creature and escapes.

Meanwhile, the three outlaws Whistler was tracking have been approached by a Mexican peasant who offers them a great deal of silver if they will use part of it to wipe out the pack of werewolves who have taken over their town. The outlaws plan to steal the silver by pretending to agree, because they not only do not believe the story, but feel no sense of obligation to live up to their words. One of them, Tucker, does seem to have a vestigial conscience, but not enough to give him a sense of honor or duty.

The escaped drunk, Hector Vargas, decides that he has a mission to destroy the werewolves, so he has some stolen silver turned into more bullets. The Mexican who recruited the threesome turns out to be a woman named Pilar, disguised as a man. The gunslingers arrive in the town and discover that it has indeed been taken over by a band of what they believe to be ordinary outlaws, except that they are clearly eating their captives. Vargas shows up too, but despite his silver bullets he is dispatched fairly easily and it is not clear what function his character really serves in the story. The gunfighters, however, successfully attack and destroy the pack, but all of the action is compressed into ten pages.

There is a fairly large plot hole. The three outlaws, we are told, turned themselves in rather than kill a federal Marshall, which prejudiced their former comrades in crime against them. That is supposedly why they are hiding in Mexico. But if they served their sentences as they say they did, there would be no reason for the bounty hunter to be looking for them, though perhaps their erstwhile comrades might be.

The novel reads like a treatment for a screenplay, with only surface description and shallow characterization. It is filled with anomalous phrases. At one point a character describes a situation as above another character's pay grade, for example, and at another point we are told "if it ain't broke, don't fix it." And later "See ya, wouldn't want to be ya." Paragraphs are short and terse – there is little texture to the prose. The story, however, is fast moving and frequently involves over the top gore. Given the author's background in movies, this is all pretty much what one might expect.

There is also a strategic problem with the novel – also common to horror films – in that none of the characters are admirable despite their last minute decision to honor their word, which makes it difficult to feel any empathy for their situation. There is virtually no suspense other than in the opening scene. The author seems to have no feel for the Old West and the anachronistic language is jarring.

Red's second horror novel is arguably science fiction. In the prologue to *It Waits Below* (2014) a meteor carrying an alien life form that exists as a controlling parasite in other types of life crashes into the Indian Ocean in 1853, sinking a Spanish treasure ship in the process. The odds against this happening are literally astronomical. A century and a half later, a private group of American entrepreneurs hopes to recover the treasure by means of a newly designed bathysphere.

Sebastian Enright is the head of the group. His crew members include Oleg Polidori, the pilot, and Jane Clark, who is being trained as Polidori's backup. They have located the sunken ship in the Marianas Trench, at a depth that would normally prohibit a diver outside the bathysphere, but in their case they have an airlock and a super-diving suit capable of withstanding the pressures at the bottom of the ocean. Sebastian's brother Roy is the more practical, less adventurous partner who keeps their business running. They have tried to keep their current project a secret because of the risk of piracy, and Roy is unhappy that another ship has been sighted in the area.

There are some minor structural problems with the early part of the story. Sebastian worries that the communications link might fail and that the surface crew would not know they were in trouble. Since this could be simply remedied by requiring positive contact at regular intervals, it is not credible that some such procedure would not be in place. Clark has a minor panic attack when she sees condensation on the inside of a porthole and assumes a leak. At that depth, any leak would be explosive and hard to miss, and it is not plausible that she would not know about condensation if she is in fact in training to be a pilot. If her knowledge was that scanty, she would not be one of the three members aboard for the crucial dive.

After a rather awkwardly written sex scene aboard the submersible, the characters reach the sunken ship. It is still recognizable despite the fact that it was struck directly by an impact so powerful that it threw fish and water two miles into the air. For reasons emphasized but never explained, they cannot use a robot to recover the sunken treasure, hence the elaborate pressure suit. Sebastian enters the wreck, is briefly out of touch, during which time his brother peremptorily announces that the project is terminated immediately, even though the brother reappears after only moments remaining incommunicado but with no indication that anything untoward has taken place.

They recover the gold with ridiculous ease but a small sea creature conceals itself in one of the bags and escapes inside the bathyscape. A creature that lived under such enormous pressure would literally explode if suddenly exposed to what we consider normal atmospheric pressure, particularly since there is no repressurization procedure, so this sequence is quite impossible.

Just before they are ready to leave, some unexplained undersea collapse traps them under wreckage of the ship and other debris and cuts off their communication. Even though the author has explicitly stated that there is no other vessel in the world that could descend to this depth, the threesome expects the surface crew to mount a rescue operation. The discussion above is equally puzzling since they now claim that there are indeed submarines that could descend to the same depth, but none of them are close enough to arrive in time. A few chapters later the author tells us once again that no rescue is possible because of the uniqueness of their equipment.

Clark decides to use the manipulator arm mounted on the submersible to dig their way out, over the irrational opposition of Polidori and Sebastian's panicky doubts. Since the only alternative is a slow death, their objections make no sense. They promptly fall over a cliff and lose the use of their engines, although somehow communications are re-established. Meanwhile, we learn that the mystery ship is run by the Russian Mafia and that they have a spy aboard the Enrights' vessel. As an aside, we are told that the Japanese navy did not have guidance systems for its torpedoes during World War II, so used suicide pilots instead. This is factually untrue; at the beginning of the war Japan had arguably the most advanced torpedoes in the world. Suicide torpedoes were rare and used only for specific missions.

The alien parasite has by now left the crab and taken possession of Polidori. The other two discover that he is infected but then the treasure ship falls on top of them, communications are lost again, and they seem to be doomed.

There is a gunfight on the surface ship as three spies are discovered among the crew – they have been communicating with the other ship by banging on their hull in Morse code! The Russians then launch an attack and seize control of the ship. Below, Clark and Enright try to subdue Polidori, but he gets the upper hand instead. After the battle goes back and forth, Polidori is killed.

The two survivors then concoct a plan by which one of them will take the diving suit, travel up to the surface, use the radio in the suit to contact the bathyscape, and then lower a line to take it in tow. But if the suit can communicate by radio with the bathyscape, why can't the surface ship do the same? And how can the suit float up when it is designed to stay down and lacks any disposable ballast? And even if they could drop the hook, how could the one left below attach it to the bathyscape when he no longer has a suit with which to go outside? Enright decides to take the chance and dies almost immediately when his suit implodes.

Another gunfight erupts on the surface ship and all of the pirates are killed. Roy Enright and the survivors recover the suit and use its radio to contact Clark, who was about to kill herself with the pistol which, for no good reason, was brought onto the submersible by Polidori. A line is dropped to retrieve the submersible, but the alien erupts from Polidori's body – a kind of bloblike creature now – so Clark leaves the bathysphere – which has by now reached a safe level in terms of pressure. Somehow she manages to swim to the surface, taking time to depressurize along the way, and reaches it successfully, even though she has no breathing equipment. The submersible is released to carry its alien passenger back down into the depths.

Clark is rather implausibly located and rescued, but one of the parasites is now attached to her leg. Another has infected a shark and sets out to spread throughout the population of sharks and whales. But before doing so it turns its current host into a giant creature and rams the surface vessel, nearly sinking it. Clark finally destroys the alien by firing a flare into an oil slick.

The novel is written like screen treatment, with little description and most of the conflict physical rather than internal. Many paragraphs are broken up into individual sentences or fragments, each given its own paragraph for no apparent reason. The protagonist's preoccupation with parts of women's bodies borders on offensiveness. There are occasional lapses into really stilted prose: "Polidori sternly scolded, his cranky voice crackling on the feed." Later: "The mechanism nearly malfunctioned and quit out several times." Although we are told that Clark is smart and competent, she acts consistently like an immature, frightened, inexperienced, and overly emotional airhead.

There is not a shred of suspense in the story despite what should be tense situations. The background detail is so implausible that it is impossible to become invested in the characters or their plight. Continuity is dreadful and the scientific content is ludicrous. The parasite tells the humans that once they have been infected, they will no longer need food or water. What then fuels their bodies? The alien is prone to uttering "shrill interstellar shrieks", whatever that might be. The author also uses meteors and asteroids interchangeably. This is an excellent example of a writer attempting to work in an area where he has little or no background.

White Knuckle (2015) avoided most of the major problems of the previous two novels and starts off reasonably well. A woman driving along the highway has her car disabled by a large truck, whose driver subsequently kills her. After this brief and relatively suspenseful opening, we meet Sharon Ormsby, an FBI agent who has specialized in highway related serial killings. She is currently investigating a series of murders involving prostitutes who hang around truck stops. The killer is a trucker who uses the handle White Knuckle, and who has a secret compartment in his rig so that he can kidnap women and murder them at his leisure before dumping their bodies. He has been doing this for thirty years.

Ormsby has a suspect but he is killed during a high speed chase. The FBI declares the case closed on that basis, which should raise an eyebrow because that would never happen either that quickly or without further investigation. And the reader, naturally, knows that this was the wrong man.

The discovery that two bodies found far apart in both time and space both have similar wounds with similar rust convinces Ormsby that they were both killed by the same person. This would be quite a leap of intuition given that the forensics could not be even close to definitive in this situation. This is a story telling shortcut that is actually unnecessary because there are other possible connections that would have been more plausible.

A kidnapping in Nebraska also seems similar – which is another major story telling leap of logic – and the FBI gets involved despite local objections – which are portrayed as short sighted but as described in the book they are both understandable and sensible. It is also unlikely that a killer who had been that successful for that long would provide details about his last victim in his radio chatter. Ormsby also acquires information from an injured witness from a case that occurred years earlier that prompts an investigation, but it would have done the same at the time given that the man knows he was assaulted by a trucker with the handle White Knuckle. Not surprisingly, Ormsby eventually is taken captive by the killer and after various travails, she manages to kill him.

Eric Red has a broad understanding of an action movie plot but appears unwilling to devote the time to ensure that the separate elements of the story are plausible. There is a consistent lack of suspense even in situations which would otherwise be tense. His prose style is terse to the point where it feels more like a summation than a narration, and none of his characters acquires any actual individuality. All three of the stories are painfully predictable in their outcomes. They are the literary equivalent of direct to video horror movies.

Norman Berrow's *The Ghost House*

Norman Berrow was a British author of more than a dozen mystery novels. *The Ghost House*, first published by Ward, Lock in 1940, was subsequently completely rewritten and reissued by St Martin's Press and Robert Hale in the United Kingdom in 1979. It is currently available as a trade paperback from Ramble House.

The story is initially established as a typical old dark house style thriller. Gerry and Jill Martin are caught in a terrible storm and when the road is partially washed away they decide to take refuge at a supposedly haunted house that they have been told has stood empty for forty years. Not far from the house they see an unconscious man lying on the shore but they are unable to carry him up the embankment, so they continue until they reach the house, which is clearly occupied after all.

Their hosts are the Ingalls, Max and Myra. Ingalls identifies himself as the son of the man who abandoned the house one night, never to be seen again, after discovering his wife's infidelity. He has just recently returned to open the house once again. Ingalls is clearly contemptuous of women and while his behavior is beyond reproach, his manner is unsettling. The butler is Carter, a surly individual who reluctantly agrees to help Martin go to the rescue of the unknown man. They bring him back to the house and when he regains consciousness, he identifies himself as Matthew Matthews and says that he was sightseeing in a small boat which capsized in the storm. There are two other guests, the Lembergs, who do not seem the kind of people whom the Ingalls would associate with, and they also behave in a mildly stilted manner.

Ingalls tells the Martins that the house is indeed haunted, but that they should not worry because none of the manifestations can do them any harm. The Martins themselves are skeptical, even when they notice that all of the mirrors have been covered or hidden. They uncover the one in the room where they are to spend the night and the image becomes cloudy and they both feel as though some supernatural power was drawing them into the mirror. Gerry breaks the spell – if that is what it was – and they cover the mirror again.

Meanwhile, the storm has brought down the power lines and the house is lit solely by candles and fireplaces.

They have a stove that uses coal for fuel so dinner is prepared and conducted in a somewhat formal fashion. Ingalls promises to tell the story of the house after they have eaten, and he proceeds to do so. His presentation is interrupted by a loud, prolonged scream from somewhere in the house, but he assures his guests that this is normal and that there is actually no one else around. The scream may be unsettling but it means nothing. He then explains that his mother either went insane or that genuine supernatural influences were at work, because she began to see things, particularly in mirrors, and sometimes other people saw apparitions or experienced other bizarre phenomena. She died one night – the scream they heard was supposedly her ghost – killed by an unknown force, although the local people believe that husband and wife had both sold their souls to the devil. The more prosaic explanation is that he threw himself into the sea – his body was never found – while she simply succumbed to guilt inspired insanity. The mother died in the same room that the Martins are to occupy, so they arrange to move to another.

The relationship between Ingalls and Carter becomes increasingly strange and it is clear that Carter does not consider himself a servant. Myra Ingalls plays the piano for a while and the Martins observe that she seems like another woman while doing so. Jill Martin falls into a deep faint and Myra succumbs similarly a moment later. They both recover but Matthews meets with the Martins later and suggests that Jill has unsuspected mediumistic powers and that was what triggered the mutual swoon. Matthews also says that he noticed that Carter was concealing fresh blood on one hand late in the evening.

Martin overhears part of a conversation between Ingalls and Carter which suggests that some mysterious plan is underway and that the three newcomers need to be watched closely During the night, Martin wakes up suddenly, realizing that someone is in the room with him. Whoever it is manages to get away unidentified, but the house is roused just in time to hear a repetition of the mysterious scream, followed by a round of laughter that appears to emanate from everywhere in the house, and which Ingalls had warned them had been heard in the past.

Carter is nowhere to be found at first but he reappears, having gone outside to investigate a noise. He informs them that the bridge has collapsed, and even if the storm subsides, they will be unable to leave in the morning. The protagonists suspect that he may have sabotaged the bridge for some reason.

The following day there is a break in the rain long enough for them to explore what is essentially an island – the only land link is a sheer cliff face. Matthews then admits to Martin that he was the intruder in their room and that he had not been sure that he could trust anyone and was checking up on the couple. Elsewhere Jill has become entranced by another mirror briefly and sees a face partially materialize. Another overheard conversation confirms that Ingalls and the others are engaged in some mysterious plot, using the ghosts – who appear to be real – as a cover. Matthews suggests some of the details by pointing out that the supposedly abandoned, eighty year old boathouse is actually much newer and smells of recent exhaust fumes, although there is no boat there at present.

Matthews convinces Jill to try to bring the face back. His theory is that the spirit wants to tell them something – possibly the location of his body if it is Ingall Senior. Each of Ingalls' parents appears briefly but since only Matthews is capable of reading lips, only he knows everything they are saying. He explains that the man made references to France and the woman was warning them to flee the house, but Martin suspects that he knows more than he is saying. Then Carter's face appears, looking confused and distraught, and after it also vanishes they search and find his dead body in one of the bedrooms.

That night when Matthews is alone with Martin, he tells him that the ghostly Ingalls told him that their host was an imposter, not Max Ingalls at all. He also admits that he saw someone signaling from a boat off shore and that the message was that someone named Ferdie would be coming ashore late in the evening. Furthermore, he is convinced that Carter deliberately wrecked the bridge on Ingalls' orders so that they would be unable to leave.

They arrange to sneak out of the house while their hosts are preoccupied with the mysterious Ferdie, but when the time comes Matthews shows up with a young woman they have never seen before, whom he identifies as a policewoman and the source of the mysterious scream. Matthews admits that he is also a police officer and tells the Martins that they stumbled into a drug smuggling and distribution operation. Their escape is not successful; Matthews is shot, the policewoman disappears and may have drowned, and the Martins are taken prisoner. Eventually they are rescued by police summoned by the policewoman, but we never learn the fate of the conspirators. Nor do we find out what happened to the body of Ingalls who disappeared forty years earlier.

There is a tradition of mystery novels that appear to have supernatural content – *Rim of the Pit* by Hake Talbot, *The Burning Court* by John Dickson Carr, *The Shadow Guest* by Evelyn Waugh, etc. – but sometimes as in this case there really is something paranormal taking place. This is somewhat problematic as a plot device because it is obviously impossible for the reader to know in advance what is rational and what is not, and that interferes with the usual compact between reader and writer in solving the puzzle. Although Berrow sorts this out and delivers a fairly good story, it works much better as a novel of the supernatural than as a crime story.

Two by the Davis Brothers

Don and Jay Davis wrote two horror novels, *Sins of the Flesh* (1989) and *Bring on the Night* (1993), then vanished from the horror field. Both books were paperback originals from Tor, which at the time had a very active, high quality horror line. The horror bust of the 1990s may have dissuaded them from further efforts.

Sins of the Flesh opens in 1938. Walter Sikes rescues his fiancé from the leader of a kind of satanic cult; the man has demonstrable supernatural powers and pronounces a curse on them that their firstborn son will be a monster. The story then jumps forward thirty years to an incident where a traveling salesman picks up a hitchhiker who grows claws and kills him. The hitchhiker sets off for the small town of Gideon, Missouri, where he had told his victim he was making a surprise visit to his parents.

Twenty more years pass. Walter Sikes is devastated when his wife suffers a stroke that will almost certainly claim her life within a few days. The couple has been keeping their son, Jesse, locked in the root cellar for two decades. Eleanor has the power to keep Jesse in an endless coma, but now that she is dying, a crisis is approaching. As her life force weakens, he wakens and the reader learns that he is essentially a werewolf, although the authors call him a wendigo. He does have the ability to seduce victims by calling to them, but he has none of the other attributes normally associated with that legend.

The viewpoint then moves to Stephen Sikes, child of Jesse's brother Isaac, now an adult. Stephen has been plagued since childhood by dreams which the reader knows refer to his inhuman uncle, although Stephen himself has no idea what inspires them. He receives a call from his grandfather about his grandmother's stroke just as Jesse arrives at the hospital and kills her, although without learning where she concealed the book of spells that enabled her to hold him captive for two decades. At the funeral, Stephen has a vision of his grandmother's corpse telling him that he must kill Jesse, whom he believes has already been dead for twenty years. That night, Jesse shows up in Stephen's bedroom and warns him to leave town.

Elsewhere the cult leader – Eugene Latham – is still at large, working a traveling revivalist tent show scam. Given his extraordinary powers, it is a bit puzzling why he would have limited himself to such penny ante activities. He is aware that Jesse is active again and decides to absent himself from his business in order to finally finish off some old business.

Jesse kills a nurse in the same over the top fashion as he did his mother because she caught a glimpse of him at the hospital. Walter tells Stephen the whole story and the two of them decide to track Jesse down and kill him. Stephen wants to search for the book of spells but Walter insists that they will never find it, and that it would not help them even if they knew where it was.

Walter shoots Jesse with a shotgun but it is ineffective and Jesse later kills him. There are several more victims who are introduced just to be slaughtered, and none of these sequences actually advances the plot. Latham confronts Jesse and tells him why he invoked the curse that created him. Jesse does not care because he likes having his powers – which later are expanded to include the ability to command snakes to do his bidding – and he tries to kill Latham, who dematerializes and escapes. Meanwhile policewoman Dana Barrows has taken a particular interest in the case and suspects that Walter and Stephen Sikes are hiding something.

Stephen eventually figures out where the book of spells is – the attentive reader will have guessed correctly long before. He steals it from where it has been hidden among the largely ignored religious books at the local library and finds a spell he believes will kill Jesse. Jesse, who can now change into the shape of other people, uses that power a couple of times before the final confrontation when Stephen successfully revives the ghosts of all of Jesse's victims, who merge into his body, somehow dissolving him into nothingness. Disappointingly, Latham escapes unscathed.

The novel betrays many of the fumbles of first novelists. Some of the minor episodes about subsidiary characters add nothing to the story and just fill space. The depiction of police operations does not ring true consistently. For example, a uniformed police officer is sent to talk to Walter Sikes following the murder. In such a high profile case – she was literally torn apart in her hospital bed – it would certainly be a detective handling the inquiries. The characterizations are relatively shallow and some questions – how did the grandmother develop her magical talents – are never really explained. Telling so much of the story from Jesse's point of view is also somewhat of a tactical error, because it reduces the element of suspense.

Unfortunately their second and final book, *Bring on the Night* (1993), was not an improvement. A mortuary technician watches as a revivified corpse – a vampire - kills two policemen, then agrees to become the vampire's familiar. Next we are introduced to Alexandra Castle, who is a genuine psychic and who does a radio show, and Detective Dennis Coglin, who is assigned to investigate the brutal murder of a nightclub owner. Elsewhere Nathan Kane, the vampire, and his wife Catherine are inspecting potential homes to buy – their appointments are all scheduled for after dark, of course. They eventually find one they like, but insist on buying the two adjoining houses as well.

After all of this is established, we meet Christian Danner, a vampire hunter, his activities interspersed with some tepid murders by Kane. Although Kane is able to control the will of others, the subsidiary vampire whom Danner questions about Kane's location apparently lacks those powers and is easily dispatched. His path crosses that of Coglin and the two eventually become partners of a sort. Danner is determined to track down Kane and Coglin wants to solve what looks like the work of a serial killer who drains the blood of his victims. Kane makes no real effort to conceal the nature of the killings, which does not seem like a very wise decision for a creature wishing to keep its true nature secret.

The story progresses slowly and the plot bears some resemblance to that of Bram Stoker's *Dracula*, with a modern setting. The morgue technician takes the place of Renfield and the psychic stands in for Mina Harker. Kane is eventually tracked down and destroyed, but Danner's work is not done as he tells Coglin that there are many more vampires yet to be eliminated.

The elements of the plot are not individually badly handled but they do not cohere very well. There is no suspense at all – we see much of the story from Kane's point of view so we know what is going to happen. There are also some odd elements, like the authors' insisting that there is a difference between psychic phenomena and the supernatural. There are too many viewpoint characters – the constant shifting is occasionally disorienting. Kane's powers are not entirely consistent and he never achieves any real stature as a villain, so his downfall is less satisfying dramatically than it might have been. This was the last collaborative effort by the brothers to see print.

Gertrude Atherton

Gertrude Franklin Horn Atherton (1857-1948) wrote more than fifty books spanning a number of genres, including fantasy and science fiction as well as horror, both supernatural and psychological. Her horror fiction was exclusively at shorter length and her two most famous stories are "The Bell in the Fog" and "The Striding Place," the latter of which she considered her best short story. She was strongly influenced by Ambrose Bierce and to a lesser extent by Henry James, but the fantastic element in her stories is often ambiguous and mental illness is a common theme. Although she was an American writer, many of her stories are set in Europe, particularly England. Her short fiction was collected in two volumes, *The Bell in the Fog and Other Stories* (1905) and The *Foghorn* (1934).

"The Bell in the Fog" is the story of Ralph Orth, an ex-patriate American novelist who acquires a mansion in England. Although he is part of the artistic set in London, he is only really happy when at his country estate. Orth becomes obsessed with two children whose paintings are in the house. He is initially told that both died young although later evidence indicates the girl lived into her twenties. A neighboring child appears to be a twin of the dead girl and he transfers his obsession to her. He attempts to adopt her but fails and eventually they part. Although there is nothing fantastic in the story, the implication is that the child is somehow privy to more than human knowledge.

In "The Striding Place" a man rescues another who has apparently fallen into a dangerous water course but when he pulls the man ashore, he discovers that the man has no face. The author provides no explanation for this and it does not seem to relate to an earlier discussion of astral projection. "The Dead and the Countess" is set in France, a small town whose cemetery is now passed quite closely by a new rail line despite the protests of the local priest that they are disturbing the dead. He hears them murmuring when he walks among the graves. There is also in that town a dying countess who dislikes life in the country and who wants to be buried near the tracks rather than in the family plot so that she can hear the train to

Paris each morning. When the priest tells the count that he hears his wife screaming in her coffin, he realizes that she was buried alive.

"The Greatest Good of the Greatest Number" describes a doctor's struggle with his conscience when he decides to allow a drug addicted woman to die so that her family will be free of her. "A Monarch of a Small Survey" is a study of a young woman trapped in the household of a domineering, ungenerous man and her tragic life following his death and the subsequent death of his widow. "The Tragedy of a Snob" is a very mundane story about a young man's reactions to snobbery.

"Crowned With One Crest" is a psychological drama about a woman who has doubts on the eve of her wedding because of a past love affair. She senses that the ghost of her earlier lover – who is still alive – is hovering about her. A woman holding vigil over her dying husband begins to fear death as a physical presence in "Death and the Woman" and when she hears what she believes to be Death's footsteps, she dies alongside her husband. "Talbot of Ursula" is a tragic romance. A rich American has long loved the wife of a business associate but remains silent even after she is widowed. On her deathbed, she realizes that she loves him.

The protagonist of "The Foghorn" is a woman who had resigned herself to a life without romance until she fell in love with a married man. Although his wife refuses him a divorce, her lover offers to run away with her to Europe and she accepts. Before they can do so, they are boating off the coast of California when a sudden fog results in an accident in which he is horribly killed before her eyes. She wakes up in what she believes to be a hospital, feeling drugged but apparently uninjured. At the end she realizes that she has been in a coma for many years and is now an old woman on the verge of death.

None of these stories are classics and only a handful include genuine supernatural events. They do share a sense of strangeness about the world, frequently as interpreted by disturbed minds.

Mrs H.D. Everett

Henrietta D. Everett (1851-1923) was a late Victorian novelist of no particular note except that she wrote a handful of short horror tales, rarely anthologized although there have been various reissues of collections under different titles.

"The Death Mask" is probably her best known story. The narrator has recently been reunited with an old friend whose wife has passed away four years previously. The wife had disapproved of the man's friends and the narrator is not unhappy to have seen the last of her. He finds his companion changed, however, unwilling to pursue a new life, to move away from the house where they lived, and reluctant to even discuss the possibility of remarrying. He explains that his wife's dying wish was that they cover her face in the coffin with a particularly handkerchief, and ever since then, attempts to pursue romance with women have been thwarted because pieces of cloth reform themselves into a death mask of his wife. The story is quite short but effectively creepy and the prose avoids the affectations common in much writing from that period.

"Parson Clench" takes place in a small English parish whose long time pastor – a very conservative man who disliked change – has recently passed away. His successor arrives to deliver his first sermon and is surprised to find himself sharing the altar area with an elderly man who remains silent and who, he learns later, is invisible to the congregation. He decides to decline the position as local pastor, a decision which is confirmed when he encounters the ghost again in the rectory. This one is a pleasantly unmelodramatic ghost story.

In "The Winds of Dunowe" Flossie Noyes, a social climber and thief, informs her husband Reginald that their successful plan to take a holiday with the MacIvors is not working out the way she had planned and she wants to cut it short. She cannot entice their young acquaintance to play cards for money and a maid stands guard over the room where Flossie believes the family jewels reside. Mrs. MacIvor, an American, is curious about the rumored ghost in the castle and Flossie decides to make use of that fact.

Her chance seems to arise when a costume party is announced. The American bride – Caryl – adopts the name of one of the family ancestors as her new identity, but perhaps coincidentally it is also the name of the family ghost, about whom no one will talk. She also cajoles her brother-in-law to let her wear the family pearls, which may only be worn by a member of the family, and which are kept secured in a safe. It is clear that there is a connection between the pearls and the ghost, Lady Slidell, although no one elaborates. Flosssie manages to steal the pearls, but a mysterious wind blows through the building, she faints, and the jewels magically reappear in the safe. The theft is never discovered.

"Nevill Nugent's Legacy" opens with a struggling couple learning that they have inherited a small estate from a cousin. One condition is that an elderly servant be allowed to live in the main house for the remainder of her life. Mrs. Wilding is helpful but the wife is immediately struck by her constant expression of hopelessness, and she herself feels a distinct sense of depression upon entering the building. She meets Wilding's husband – he is an invalid incapable of walking named Thomas Bassett – and dislikes him immediately. The feeling is apparently mutual because Mrs. Wilding has reverted to her maiden name.

The wife also sees a young boy in the area, but he disappears mysteriously and she decides that he must be a ghost. Mrs. Wilding admits that other people have seen the figure – although she has not – but insists that there is no reason or such a ghost to inhabit the house. She then admits that her own son disappeared at about the right age but he had told her that he was running away to sea to get away from Bassett, his step father. The reader is likely to correctly conclude from this that Bassett killed the boy before he could leave, and when some alterations are being made to the house, his bones are discovered.

"The Crimson Blind" describes the experiences of two cousins who decide to spend a night in a supposedly haunted house. One of them is firmly convinced that it is all a prank and that a third cousin will perpetrate some manifestation designed to frighten him with the connivance of his companion. Before they can enter the house, a figure appears at the window and jumps through it. They run off in panic, joined by the third boy who was indeed intent upon hoaxing his cousin. A death in the family and other circumstances prevent any of them from returning during the daylight to find out what has happened.

Twenty years pass. The young man is now in his thirties and looking for a wife. He meets a young woman and accepts an invitation to visit her family, unaware that it is the same house, which he does not recognize since it has been redecorated. That night he wakens, sees the window of his room in its old guise, but falls asleep again. In the morning he believes it to have been a dream. He does, however, believe that this was the same house he visited as a youth. He tells his host after the vision is repeated, but the latter scoffs. Several months later, the family is forced to move away because the servants have been frightened off by the ghost of a mental patient who died in that very room.

"Fingers of a Hand" is a very short piece in which a disembodied hand materializes to warn the residents of a cottage of an imminent landslide. "Anne's Little Ghost" concerns a couple who encounter what might be a ghost, but turns out to be something else, a kind of manifestation generated by the house they are inhabiting rather than the spirit of a dead person. A man receives telephone calls from his dead fiancé in "Over the Wires," but her end of the conversation was while she was alive, though dying, and with no access to a telephone.

Richard Quinton is "The Next Heir." He is the last male descendant of the Canadian branch of his family and the last of his English relatives is an invalid who wishes to meet him and determine whether or not to name him heir to his estate. Several of the standard devices of the ghost story occur quickly – strange music in the darkness, a vision of two men fighting, and a dream in which he sees a woman pacing his bedroom restlessly. He also learns that his host is obsessed with pagan rites supposedly practiced in the area during the time of the Roman occupation.

His host contends that Pan was a descendant of Cain and that Cain was a better man than his brother. He also demonstrates that Quinton has some latent psychic power, but this distresses Quinton severely. Subsequently he learns that the man's mother blamed him for the death of his brother – reflecting the Cain and Abel dichotomy – and that he bleeds through the pores of his hands from time to time as a kind of stigmata. Quinton refuses to be named heir and leaves, but his cousin dies suddenly, intestate, so he inherits anyway, although he is not bound to any of the conditions originally attached to the estate and in fact he promptly has the pagan restoration removed and prepares to sell the property. But first he sneaks back one night, intent upon burning the house to the ground, in which task he succeeds after some mild adventures.

The narrator of "A Water Witch" is the sister of a married man who agrees to keep his wife company while he is away on business. Shortly after arriving, she learns that one of the local farmers has lost several animals that year, all of whom were drowned in the nearby river. The wife explains that there is a legend of a drowned woman whose spirit lures the animals in, but it seems more likely that the inadequate fencing is the explanation. The narrator experiences some of these phenomena but rather obtusely fails to listen when the wife expresses a desire to leave immediately. Although they both survive the final crisis, the wife dies a few months later, having been weakened by her ordeal.

"The Lonely Road" is a very short tale of a man defended by a ghostly dog when he is accosted by two thieves. A man sees another ghostly figure in "A Girl in White", but can uncover no legend of a ghost or even the existence of a young girl in the area. He finds a possible solution to the mystery but is never quite certain. "A Perplexing Case" concerns two soldiers hospitalized with shell shock who temporarily switch bodies.

"Beyond the Pale" pits a British couple against a witch in an unidentified foreign land. The witch curses them and they undergo some frightening and inexplicable events before they find another who reverses the spell. In "The Pipers of Mallory" a new bride whose husband is off to fight in the war in Europe reluctantly travels to Scotland to visit the mother-in-law she has never met and whom she is predisposed to dislike. Even before arriving she learns that the older woman disdains bagpipes and does not have a piper on her estate, which seems odd. While walking on the grounds, the visitor hears a ghostly piping and then learns that the sound of pipes is heard whenever one of the family is about to die. The legend proves to be true. ""The Whispering Wall" is very short involving another ghostly premonition of death.

Everett was a talented writer whose prose style is relatively modern. Most of her ghost stories are quite conventional, but there are some which have the same kind of magical flavor as some of the best work of Algernon Blackwood. Most of these stories appear to have been written shortly after World War I. Although it is unlikely that she would ever have achieved the stature of a major author, her work is comparable in quality to writers like H. Russell Wakefield and Oliver Onions.

The Aylmer Vance Stories

Alice Askew (1874-1917) and Claude Askew (1865-1917) were a prolific husband and wife writing team who turned out around ninety books during their career, plus assorted shorter work. The Aylmer Vance series was their only supernatural work of note and it was collected by Ash-Tree Press in 1998 and reprinted by Wordsworth in 2006. The Askews died when the ship on which they were traveling was torpedoed during World War I.

Aylmer Vance is a detective of the occult, that is, he tends to investigate incidents of the supernatural. His friend – an attorney named Dexter – is the narrator of his adventures, a kind of Watson to Aylmer's Holmes, although Dexter has some clairvoyant powers that make him more important to the plot than was Watson's usual role. In their first appearance, "The Invader," Dexter asks Vance to describe some of his previous investigatory work as a member of the Ghost Circle, which concerned itself with the occult. They have only been acquainted for about two months on this occasion and have yet to work together.

Vance is described as a loner, a bachelor who travels as great deal but who does not make friends easily. Dexter is fascinated by him and is determined to further their acquaintance. Vance describes himself as primarily a debunker of frauds and a student of unexplained but natural phenomena although he admits that on a few occasions he has been at a loss to provide a rational explanation. He agrees to relate the story of the Sinclair tragedy, which was instrumental in convincing him to devote his life to investigation supposedly supernatural events.

George Sinclair was Vance's closest friend and the latter was pleased to attend the wedding in which he married Annie Riddell. The bride is beautiful but seems lacking in personality and after a few months of marriage it is obvious that she is completely under his domination, although for his part he is devoted and kind. The couple remained childless and, perhaps as compensation, George eventually became interested in occult research in general and an ancient barrow on his property in particular. George becomes convinced that his wife has mediumistic powers and insists upon putting her into trances.

George believes – and Vance apparently concurs – that his wife genuinely was in contact with the unhappy spirit of a British princess who had been interred in the barrow. The princess announces that she is in love with George and that she would like to acquire permanent possession of Annie's body. Vance advises him to stop before something unfortunate takes place, but George continues until Annie herself refuses, insisting that it has become increasingly difficult to regain control of her own body after each session.

She finally agrees to one final sitting, and this time the disembodied spirit refuses to leave. For weeks she occupies Annie's body, displaying cruelty and savagery so intense that the servants all give notice. Eventually George, despairing, kills Annie – or rather her body – and then himself. Vance admits that he could construct a rational, psychological explanation of what happened, but asserts that he believes this really was a case of possession. The reader must decide independently.

The second story in the series was "The Stranger." Daphne Darrell was Vance's cousin's child and he became her guardian after the cousin drowned and his wife died giving birth to Daphne. Daphne was rather a tomboy and she also had what everyone thought was an imaginary friend, a young man whom she met in the woods, and from whom she was for a time inseparable.

She grows to adulthood and becomes engaged. Vance is delighted with her choice of fiancé, but startled when she insists that she actually loves the imaginary companion of her childhood, whom she still sees from time to time. He is clearly the manifestation of a Greek god and on the day before the wedding, Vance sees Daphne encounter him in the forest, and then she is dead, apparently struck by lightning. It is a disappointing though perhaps inevitable conclusion.

"Lady Green-Sleeves" is a ghostly girl who appeared at a fancy dress party when Vance was much younger. He was fascinated but most people could not see her and no one managed to get close enough to talk to her before she disappeared. They talk and she disappears, having just manifested herself out of curiosity about how the world had changed since her death. There is not much to this one.

"The Fire Unquenchable" is the first in which Dexter is not just the passive listener to Vance's stories. Vance asks him to read a manuscript, a collection of poems, and share his opinion of them. This is also the story in which Dexter discovers that he is clairvoyant, because while reading the poems he has a vision of a young romantic couple and feels intense heat as though he was near a fire. The next day Vance tells him that the author took his own life in despair when he could not find a publisher, leaving the woman he loved alone in the world. After his death, small fires would inexplicably spring up in the house he used to occupy. He had destroyed all of his work before his death, but Vance had convinced his widow to help reconstruct them by means of automatic writing.

At the beginning of "The Vampire," we are told that Dexter and Vance are now living together. One of their first joint clients is a man named Paul Davenant. Davenant has been suffering from a mysterious loss of blood which his doctors cannot explain and he has an unusual new scar on his neck. This had been going on for six months and he was desperate to find an explanation. His description of his recent experiences clearly indicate to the reader that he is the victim of nocturnal feedings by a vampire.

Davenant is in love with Jessica MacThane, a young woman with a striking physical appearance. Jessica resists his proposals, telling him that her family is cursed and that she is determined to be the last of her line. The curse does not affect her family directly but rather causes anyone who is intimate with them to waste away and die. The curse originated with an ancestor whom Jessica is thought to resemble, who disappeared and was probably murdered by neighbors who believed her to be a witch.

At first the new couple lives happily together, but they pay a visit to the old family castle and shortly thereafter Jessica finds it impossible to leave without becoming horribly ill. Vance and Dexter accompany Davenant back to the castle where Vance determines that it is the spirit of the ancient witch and not Jessica who has been preying on the sleeping man. He breaks the spell and the couple leaves the castle, which is to be demolished in order to finally lay her ghost to rest. This is a better than average vampire story with a twist at the end.

"The Boy of Blackstock" has the duo investigating poltergeist phenomena associated with a family curse. Lord Rystone lives with his wife, two sons by a previous marriage, and their tutor. He is stubborn, arrogant, and domineering. The haunting is connected to a particular room and Vance decides to spend a night there alone. Dexter then overhears the tutor trying to blackmail the wife because he knows that she has a secret lover who is behind the poltergeist tricks. Rystone discovers the truth but just as he is about to shoot the two lovers, he is accosted by the genuine ghost and falls dead.

Vance and Dexter answer a friend's summons in "The Indissoluble Bond." Colonel Verriker is concerned about his daughter Beryl. Beryl, who is engaged to be married, has experienced periods in which she appears to be listening to something inaudible to everyone else, after which she retreats to her room with a supposed headache, although on at least one occasion she has promptly sneaked out of the house instead. The incidents appear to have stopped by the time Vance arrives.

Vance learns that Beryl had recently been taking organ lessons from a local man. Coincidentally, the lessons have been suspended because the instructor, Cuthbert Ford, has been ill. This period coincides perfectly with the period during which Beryl has been acting normally, a situation which is about to change once again.

When Dexter notices that Beryl has succumbed to a fresh attack, he informs Vance. The reader is then given a demonstration of Dexter's clairvoyance when Vance puts him into a trance so that he can astrally project himself and follow the young woman. In that form he witnesses a conversation between Beryl and Ford in which the latter asserts that he has the power to control her soul and that he is unwilling to surrender that power. Ford promises not to call her again during his lifetime, but he dies shortly thereafter and summons her during her wedding, to the dismay of all concerned including Vance. The conclusion is somewhat ambiguous and the central conflict remains unresolved.

The final story in the sequence was "The Fear." Vance's last client is a businessman who recently bought and refurbished a country manor. He and his family were forced to move out because they felt a formless, mysterious sense of terror at odd moments, even though there was never any apparent cause. Inquiries turn up no rumors of anything untoward among the local people.

Shortly after arriving at the house, both Vance and Dexter experience brief moments of abject terror. They eventually discover that there is in fact a story about previous owners, including fratricide and insanity. Their conclusion is that the house must be torn down and replaced because the emotions and spirits of the past have become rooted in physical structures and cannot be otherwise removed.

The series is pleasant but unexceptional. The investigative work is minimal and while Vance always figures out what the root cause of the problem is, he can almost never do anything about it. Dexter's clairvoyance is only invoked when it is convenient. "The Invader" and "The Vampire" are the best of them.

William H. Hallahan

William H. Hallahan (born 1925) has for most of his career been a writer of thrillers and crime novels, but for a brief period he turned his attention to horror, producing two excellent and one readable novels in that genre. His first, *The Search for Joseph Tully* (1974) enjoys a small but lingering reputation for its creepy atmosphere and suspense but by the mid-1980s Hallahan had reverted to more mundane suspense.

The Search for Joseph Tully opens in late 15th Century Rome where a set of two blades, a rapier and a stiletto, are in the process of being forged. The forging is completed when each blade is used to brutally kill one of a pair of captives prepared for that purpose. The story than moves forward to the present.

A man named Peter Richardson is disturbed while sleeping by the sound of something like a golf club being swung through the air, but there is no one else in his apartment. In the apartment directly below is Albert Clabber, who has been excommunicated from the Roman Catholic Church for heresy and who has in turn issued a writ of excommunication for the church itself. Two rooms away from Richardson is the apartment of Oswaldo Goulart, an artist. Their building is slated to be demolished and they are all looking for new apartments. Another neighbor is Abigail Withers, an elderly woman who is a close friend of Clabber and Richardson. Withers, among others, has seen lights in one of the abandoned buildings, lights which the police have investigated without discovering who or what was responsible. Their own building has been condemned and they have only weeks to find new homes before they are evicted.

Richardson has acquired the sudden conviction that someone is going to kill him. He has no evidence for his fear, but he is quite certain. Elsewhere in New York City a man named Matthew Willow has just arrived from England and is moving into an apartment. Willow is searching for someone named Joseph Tully and consults with a genealogist, trying to trace the family tree. Clearly the two incidents are connected somehow.

Richardson is friends with Griselda Vandermeer, who claims to have occult powers. He accompanies her to a party in the building where a tarot reader named Quist seems oddly unwilling to do a reading for him. A short while later, Goulart mysteriously disappears from his apartment. Worried, Richardson consults with Clabber, who asks him if he has been hearing an inexplicable sound. Richardson reluctantly tells him about the swishing noise, but refuses to discuss it further.

Richardson suspects that someone is putting drugs in his food which are causing him to hallucinate. A medical examination eliminates that possibility and he next wonders if his auditory hallucination is just the result of stress. A detective shows up to look into Goulart's disappearance, but when Richardson tries to check back with him, he learns that the man was killed in the line of duty twenty years earlier. Goulart's body turns up at last, frozen stiff in one of the condemned buildings. The walls in this building are filled with phantasmagoric paintings, monks in cowls, strange plants and animals, demons, and a flaming sword. The only writing on the wall is an admonition for Richardson to run for his life.

Clabber tells Richardson that Goulart had been experimenting with the occult and with drugs, and that recently he had indicated that he thought Richardson's life was in danger. He also makes reference to a 16th Century Italian heretic named Giordano Bruno, who believed in reincarnation. This is the first hint we have about the reason for Willow's attempts to track down Tully's descendants. Richardson continues to dither about moving, but one evening he goes down to the basement to feed Goulart's now orphaned cat and finds a room he had never seen before. Inside is a man with a tape recorder playing the sound Richardson has been hearing. He returns to his apartment in a panic, then arms himself with a makeshift weapon and goes back to investigate, but the room appears to have vanished. Or did he just imagine it?

Clabber convinces Richardson to attend a séance which tells him nothing but leaves him upset. Later that night he makes a surprise visit to Clabber's new apartment and catches him with the man who claimed to be the dead police detective, but who is instead the son of that man. Richardson begins to panic and quickly rents a new apartment but before he can leave, Clabber convinces him to submit to hypnosis, under which he identifies himself as Joseph Tully.

In the closing pages we discover that Joseph Tully is the reincarnation of the man who ordered the two men killed in the prologue. Willow is the reincarnation of his enemy, who has pursued him through various incarnations in order to wreak vengeance. The story ends as Willow, now armed with a sword, ascends the staircase toward Clabber and Richardson.

Hallahan interweaves three story lines to provide constant momentum – the demolition of the neighborhood, Richardson's strange experiences, and Willow's attempts to trace all of the descendants of Joseph Tully for reasons unknown. He uses a tight, terse style with considerable dialogue and minimal description, and this enables him to distinguish his characters by their personalities rather than their physical characteristics. Although reincarnation had become a standard horror trope by this time, Hallahan infuses new life into it by obscuring what is really happening until the final scene. It was a very promising debut horror novel.

Hallahan's second novel of the supernatural was *Keeper of the Children* (1978). Fourteen year old Renni Benson and a companion fail to come home from school one night. When her father, Eddie Benson, returns from a photoshoot in Europe, he learns from his wife Susan that the two girls have joined a cult gathered around the figure of Tran Cao Kheim, who claims to be a Vietnamese refugee and Buddhist monk whose life is dedicated to purchasing food for the starving people of Asia. In fact, the money raised by his minions seems to be going primarily to support his elegant life style and he is clearly a fraud.

Several of the affected parents have banded together in an effort to recover their children. The head of the group is Kenneth Custis, who hired a private detective to look into Kheim's past. This resulted in a report that charges that Kheim is an imposter who entered the country illegally, and that he is actually from Tibet. Custis believes that this can be used to deport the cult's leader, but that the process will drag on unless the report is personally delivered to the responsible officials with an explanation about why fast action is desirable.

This plan is disrupted when a scarecrow comes to life and kills Custis in his own home, in full view of several of the other parents. The scarecrow collapses after accomplishing its mission. Some of the witnesses refuse to believe the evidence of their own eyes and some are so frightened that they disengage from the group. Eddie is one of those who remains determined to get his daughter back.

Another father announces his intention of carrying through with the deportation plan, and he has locked himself in a supposedly impregnable room with barred windows to protect himself from rampaging scarecrows. He dies that night when a band of cats controlled by Kheim slip through the bars of the windows and tear him apart.

The situation escalates quickly. One of the mothers – despondent – has apparently committed suicide, but her obnoxious husband is murdered by an animated manikin, even though he has no interest in getting his estranged daughter back. This warns Eddie that he may be on the target list. He creates an elaborate trap to catch any magical intruder but when one of his daughter's dolls come to life, he narrowly avoids being killed. In the process of defending himself he forces the animating force out of the doll where it manifests itself as a small dark cloud of freezing cold.

From this he concludes that Kheim astrally projects himself, then uses psychokinesis to bring inanimate things to temporary life. He concludes that the only possible defense is to learn to astrally project himself and meet Kheim on the other plane of existence. He contacts an adept who reluctantly agrees to try to teach him to enter the astral plane in order to combat the evil spirit of Kheim.

After a few days of training, rather implausibly, Benson is able to leave his body and animate objects. His first confrontation with Kheim ends with a draw, and he has lost the element of surprise by revealing his new abilities. Ultimately Benson wins by severing the cord that anchors Kheim to his body.

This was not nearly as interesting a story as *The Search for Joseph Tully*, even though the narration is tighter and the prose more detailed. For one thing, the police are only mentioned in passing despite the spate of violent deaths and they would have been far more evident under these bizarre circumstances, and probably accompanied by a crowd of journalists. Nor is child welfare or any other agency particularly interested in the cult, despite the fact that it consists of minor children, at least two of whom now have babies of their own. Nor is it particularly believable that the protagonist should – in a short period of time – master occult powers with enough skill to counter an adept who had been studying them for decades.

Hallahan's third and last horror novel was *The Monk* (1983). Monks appear in all three of the novels, images of them painted on walls in the first, a Tibetan monk as chief villain, and now the third. The book opens with a retelling of the story of the war in Heaven, the fall of Lucifer, and adds a twist. Timothy, who rebelled but repented, is to perpetually wander the Earth until he finds a baby with a purple aura. When the baby matures, he must convince the adult to forgive his sins. To prevent this from happening, Lucifer – now known as Satan – is present on Earth in the form of an immortal hawk with magical powers. He reaches each infant first and kills it before the prophecy can be fulfilled.

After the lengthy prologue, Brendan Davitt is born with a purple aura, and a banshee wails at his birth, which is unprecedented. His mother has second sight but his powers of precognition manifest themselves early and they are much more impressive. He is hidden from both powers who seek him because an order of monks temporarily changes his aura's color, although this will wear off at some time in the future.

Brendan's childhood is troubled. He has dreams of a horrible figure on a black horse which is clearly Satan. His mother had visions of a monk with a white dog, which was probably Timothy. Friends and family members are unsettled by his ability to predict deaths and largely avoid him. In his teens, his parents are killed in an automobile accident and he goes to live with his aunt. While attending college, he decides that his visions are real and attempts to find someone who can help him prepare for what is to come, but his fears are largely dismissed as fantasy. Meanwhile, the surviving monks who helped him as an infant are trying to find him because they know that his true nature will be revealed soon and they want to hide him in a monastery where he may or may not be safe.

The struggle continues with both sides seeking Brendan. Ultimately, of course, Timothy perseveres and is forgiven in the name of all humanity. Satan retreats to Hell and decides to launch an assault on Heaven as a desperate last gamble, only to find that Heaven and Earth have both now been withdrawn from any plane of existence that he or his minions can enter. It is his ultimate defeat.

The premise is very shaky for this story. In order to provide some chance that Brendan will survive, the author has to make both Satan and Timothy so fallible that they seem quite human and therefore not particularly menacing. In fact, during the prologue the war in Heaven is so mundane that everyone involved, including God, is portrayed as inept, inconsiderate, and self obsessed. Despite Brendan's visions, there is very little tension for the first half of the novel, and the presence of a group of monks who just happen to know how to change the color of someone's aura just as he is being born is more than slightly too convenient.

Hallahan also had a short horror story in Modern Masters of Horror edited by Frank Coffey in 1981, "The New Tenant." The protagonist has just married his late partner's wife and this is the first night he is spending in her house. He wakes up hearing as strange rapping sound, after which he has a frightening dream of being pursued through a maze of rooms by someone who wants to ferret out his secrets and make them public. His opponent turns out to be the dead partner's spirit, who takes control of his body in order to return to life with the woman he loves obsessively. She knows what is going on and is worried that the displaced spirit might be able to recover control of the body, but her reborn husband reassures her that he is on guard and that it is impossible. Later that same night, the bodiless spirit does return, and seizes control of the wife's body, separating the couple once again. The story has a nice twist, but Hallahan does not seem to have favored short stories.

LOUISA BALDWIN

Louisa MacDonald Baldwin (1845-1925) was the Scottish born mother of Stanley Baldwin who served as prime minister of Great Britain. She was married to a business entrepreneur and wrote a number of novels, short stories, and poems, although she never became a popular figure. She wrote only ten stories of the supernatural, which have been collected as *The Shadow on the Blind and Other Stories*. Her work is somewhat formulaic, but her prose is crisp and clear and ages quite well.

The title story is her best known work. It opens with an evocative description of Harbledon Hall, which has been deserted for seven years and is rapidly turning into a ruin. An elderly man named Stackpoole is taken by the appearance of the Hall and decides that it would be a rewarding project to restore it to its former glory. His wife is less thrilled by the prospect for she has seen him indulge it before. Once the restoration is complete, her husband loses interest and begins searching for another crumbling edifice.

This particular house was abandoned quite suddenly by Sir Roland Shawe and his family, who left without explanation even though their lease still had five years remaining. The local deacon suggests that they were driven away by ghosts, although that had in fact remained in residence for sixteen years prior to their abrupt departure. Stackpoole is predictably skeptical, although his wife feels that there is something odd about the building.

There are no disturbances during the restoration or the early days of occupancy and Stackpoole is confident that electric light and other modern conveniences have banished the shadows and uncertainties that have in the past led to what he believes to be delusions about ghostly interventions. To celebrate the opening of their new home, the Stackpooles stage an elaborate costume ball. The reader is clearly being prepared for an event that will come amidst the celebration.

As expected a handful of people observe the reenactment of an old murder. The shadows of two struggling men are seen at one window, and one stabs the other with a sword. Stackpoole himself hears the struggle from the room directly below, and his daughter sees one of the figures in the corridor. He and his family leave

Harbledon Hall the next day, never to return. This is the classic form of the ghost story, with no one suffering any actual physical harm, but the protagonists so frightened that they are driven away.

"The Weird of the Walfords" deals with the haunted object rather than the haunted house. The protagonist/narrator has for much of his life had a dread of an oversized bed where his mother died, and upon inheriting the family house, he immediately has it cut into pieces and removed from the house. His justification is that the prospect of dying in that bed as did many of his ancestors seems to him a form of imposed predestination. "Must this ghastly horror of my childhood be the goal towards which I tend?"

Walford's neighbors and servants both consider him eccentric in the wake of this act of destruction, but he is not disturbed by the notion. He even allows one of the servants to carry off some of the carved panels from the bed. But at last he begins to grow lonely and takes an American wife. The room where the bed once stood has been locked and out of use but she decides that it should be made over into a sitting room, despite his inarticulate objection.

Walford refuses to unlock the room until his wife looks through the keyhole and sees a bed. He opens the door to prove that it is empty, and then agrees to leave it unlocked, so long as she makes no effort to furnish it. She becomes pregnant and purchases a rocking cradle in the local town, and to Walford's horror it has been constructed using the same panels that he gave away when the bed was being dismantled. Predictably, the baby dies shortly after being placed in the cradle.

To ease the pain for his distraught wife, Walford allows her to turn the fatal chamber into a sitting room and a few months later she dies there, presumably succumbing to her grief. Walford then sends all of the servants away and burns his ancestral home to the ground. Although there are no actual ghosts, this is a story about a haunting, a cursed object that has acquired its menace from the succession of deaths that occurred in its vicinity.

"The Uncanny Bairn" takes a different tack and contains a good deal of dialect which makes sometimes difficult reading. A farming couple gives birth to a sickly baby who manages to survive to be eight years old. Symptomatic of attitudes at the time the story was written, the parents are careful not to tell the boy any ghost stories or anything suggesting the fantastic because the doctor has warned them that any fright or upset could cause a severe deterioration of the boy's health. But one day he visits an old woman and innocently foretells her death, which takes place three days later. It is assumed that the boy has second sight, a kind of blend of precognition and clairvoyance.

The boy's father is alarmed because he has experience of another family member, now dead, whose ability to predict death made her an object of considerable bad feeling. His predictions continue to be accurate until he sees his own father's death, after which the power seems to have left him, perhaps because of the approach of adolescence. Like many stories of this type, it has no real resolution or conclusion but rather is simply a description of mildly unsettling events that seem to follow no real pattern.

"Many Waters Cannot Quench Love" opens with a familiar device, a brief passage assuring us that the main character is a man of veracity and lacking in imagination. In this case he rents a remote cottage in order to enjoy some time in the country. He takes up residence with the caretaker and her adult son as his only companions. The former residents were a family named Maitland who are sailing to a new life in Australia. Their oldest daughter is engaged to a young farmhand who is to join them the following year, but he is presently worried about the dangers of their journey. One night the protagonist has a vision of a young woman weeping in the cottage, but she disappears. The following morning he learns that the farmhand fell into the river and drowned during the night, and some time later reads in the paper that the ship carrying his lover was lost with all hands on the very same evening. This use of dramatic coincidence is another staple of the ghost story.

"How He Left the Hotel" is a vignette about an elevator operator who discovers that the man he brought down to the lobby an hour earlier actually died and is still in his bed upstairs. "My Next Door Neighbor" is a recounting of the narrator's prolonged stay at a hospital and his acquaintance with a man from Breton in France. The other man is dying and toward the end the ghost of the woman he loves – who died years earlier – appears at his bedside. This was not one of Baldwin's better efforts. The buildup is slow and meandering and entirely disproportionate to the very brief climax.

In "The Real and the Counterfeit" three young men are enjoying a winter holiday together in the home of one whose family has gone abroad. The host, Musgrave, tells them that there is technically a family ghost, actually the spirit of a monk who died in the cloister that was razed in order to build the house. No one in the family has seen him in generations but the legend has persisted. One of the guests – who does not believe in ghosts – decides to play a practical joke designed to convince his two companions that they have indeed seen the spirit of the monk. Once again, quite predictably, the prank goes awry when the real ghost appears, and the prankster is literally frightened to death by the apparition. It was unusual for supernatural visions to actually result in physical harm in Victorian ghost stories.

"The Empty Picture Frame" is a rather flat story in which an aging spinster invites a cousin to visit her ancestral home. A woman appears who seems to be the cousin but who bears an uncanny resemblance to a woman who died generations earlier and whose painting has disappeared from its frame. There is no mystery about the explanation – the ghost of the woman has animated the portrait and brought it to life – and the story wanders to an end rather a conclusion.

The narrator of "Sir Nigel Otterburne's Case" is a medical student who is asked to help monitor the health of Sir Nigel, whose malaria has metamorphosed into an anomalous form. He is a widower with an adult daughter who is distinctly cool to her father's physicians. Both the patient and his daughter are convinced, rightly, that he is dying and that no medical efforts will help. During his final moments, the ghosts of his ancestors all appear in the courtyard and with them is the ghost of his son, who was believed to be still among the living.

The last of Baldwin's stories is "The Ticking of the Clock." It is not clear that it has any fantastic content. A young boy believes that his grandfather is ageing because of the ticking of a clock, and when he stops the clock, his grandfather dies. None of these stories could be considered even minor classics of the horror genre, but they are generally well constructed and well told tales of the supernatural.

LETTICE GALBRAITH

Little is known about Victorian writer Lettice Galbraith, who produced one completely forgotten mundane novel and a handful of short stories of the supernatural. Galbraith's prose is sometimes rather labored, but her plots tend to be reasonably inventive and sometimes even clever.

"The Case of Lady Lukestan" is a case in point. The Lady of the title had conducted a mild flirtation with a clergyman who, not being of sound mind, concluded that she wished to marry him. When she turned him down, he vowed some unspecified revenge and a short time later took his own life. She is secretly married – hence her assumed title – but her husband dies before the union can be formally proclaimed and the clergyman who performed the ceremony, brother of the suicide, asserts that no such wedding ever took place.

A lawyer finds evidence that the wedding really happened but that the signature of the officiating pastor is that of the dead man. This results in a court case in which her legal counsel attempts to convince the jury that it was a legal marriage, but since English law does not recognize the existence of ghosts, the decision is against her.

"The Trainer's Ghost" is quite good. A band of men who make a living fixing horse races believe that their latest plot is going to be thwarted thanks to a mysterious new colt that has just been entered in a race. They decide to sabotage its chances by making a late night visit to the stables, but the colt is being kept in a stall where one of the trainers was kicked to death years earlier. When they overcome the man on guard and enter the cell, they are confronted by the ghost of the dead trainer.

"The Ghost in the Chair" opens with a somewhat different structure. We are told in the opening paragraph what is essentially the climax of the story – a man seen to be attending a business meeting hours after his death. Curtis Yorke is chairman of the board of a mining company which has had a run of recent reversals. He is described as a brilliant man who seems to have lost his touch, but also a very superstitious one. Yorke unwisely remarked to his associates that he would sell his very soul in order to save the company from financial ruin.

On a whim, he writes up a contract to that effect, but to his horror a cryptic signature appears on the paper just before he throws it into the fire. A few days later he addresses the board, then mysteriously disappears, and it is learned later that he had already been dead for several hours. The story suffers a bit from its prolonged denouement, which repeats information already conveyed and belabors several points that were better left implied.

"In the Séance Room" features an ambitious and unscrupulous young doctor who has made a minor reputation for himself by dabbling in hypnotism and other occult matters. He is about to be married to a wealthy young woman and has covered up a past indiscretion – which resulted in pregnancy – by having the woman disappear. In fact the police recover a body from the Thames that they identify as the missing young lady and he finds the irony of their error quite amusing.

He is disturbed one night when his mistress shows up on his doorstep in an obvious state of distress. It occurs to him then that her real death would solve all of his problems, so he stages his faked attempt to rescue her while drowning. With his difficulties apparently ended, he marries and four years later is enjoying a very successful career and social life. He exploits those who believe in the occult although he privately considers it nonsense.

While attending a séance on the anniversary of the murder, he receives a communication which is clearly from the dead woman, after which the ring that he lost during the faked rescue attempt mysteriously reappears. That night his wife secretly hypnotizes him and draws out the entire story. Facing disgrace and ruin, he takes his own life.

"The Missing Model" is set in the world of the artist. A painter is lamenting the fact that his best model has gotten married and declared herself no longer available to pose. A fellow artist recounts another case where a model mysteriously disappeared while walking from her home to an artist's studio, never to be heard from again. He also recommends another model and a woman shows up a short time later, but the artist/protagonist later discovers that she is not the person he had been expecting. In fact, someone recognizes her face in his painting. She is the same woman who disappeared a year earlier. She makes another appearance before finally revealing the resting place of her body, for she was murdered and secretly buried the day she disappeared.

In "A Ghost's Revenge" Gerald Harrison agrees to spend a few days visiting an old friend in the country. There he meets a neighbor, Granville, who is clearly greatly stressed. The friend tells Harrison that Granville believes the house in which he lives is haunted. A few hours later Granville is found dead, having drowned in a pond near his house. Several years later Harrison answers a desperate summons from his old friend. He finds his friend in a coma and helps save him from ghostly revenge, although he will never again be the man he once was.

"The Blue Room" is probably Galbraith's best known story, although it is quite short. Once again we are told plainly in the opening paragraph that a genuine ghost is involved. The narrator is a servant hired at a hall whose mysterious Blue Room has a bad reputation. No one talks about it but everyone assumes that it is frequented by a ghost. She learns that a family member died there years earlier, a woman whose morals were suspect and who was buried apart from the rest of the family.

The occasion of an extended party brings a crisis because one of the guests unexpectedly brings a companion and the Blue Room is the only one still available. The following morning she is found dead with her eyes open and staring.

Fifty years later, the narrator is still working at the estate and the Blue Room has been closed up since the tragedy. A young woman named Edith Erristoum is a houseguest and she insists that there are no such things as ghosts. When she hears the story, she vows to sleep in the Blue Room that very night, but she is forestalled by a male guest who insists on doing so first. His stay in the room is completely uneventful.

A ghostly figure appears to Erristoum but she is saved by the intervention of the narrator and two men who were keeping watch. The specter vanishes but Erristoum recalls a dreamlike memory of a secret panel and they search for it. They find a document linked to a magical spell and destroy it, thus banishing the ghost forever. This was clearly Galbraith's best story. Had she been more prolific, she might well be better known today, but with such a small body of work, she is most likely to remain nothing more than an interesting minor figure.

IN GHOSTLY COMPANY

Amyas Northcote (1864-1923) was an English writer who served both as a justice of the peace in England and a businessman in the United States. He wrote a handful of short stories – mostly about ghosts – which were collected as *In Ghostly Company* in 1921. He attended Oxford contemporaneously with M.R. James to whom his work is sometimes compared. He died shortly after the book was published.

Possibly the most memorable of his stories was "Brickett Bottom", which has been occasionally anthologized. The story opens with Parson Maydew and his two adult daughters, Alice and Maggie, traveling to take up temporary resident in a country parish. The title refers to a meadow past which the sisters are walking one day when Alice spies a house in the distance, a house which is invisible to her sister. Maggie turns her ankle and is unable to walk about but Alice returns the next day and reports that the house is neatly constructed and occupied by an older couple to whom she nodded but who did not speak.

Alice has intermittent odd dreams about the house, which she secretly visits from time to time while Maggie is confined to the house by her injury. One day she admits that the woman of the house spoke to her, identified the man as the retired Colonel Paxton, and invited Alice to come in, although she was late getting home and declined to accept the invitation. She announces her intention to pay a longer visit the following day.

When Alice does not return at the time promised, Maggie speaks to her father, who is clearly displeased. He orders a cart readied and he and Maggie are conveyed to the spot where, predictably, there is no house to be found, although they do briefly hear Alice calling to them. Their servant insists that he has never heard of a house at the meadow, nor does he know of anyone named Paxton.

Alice is never found, but the Maydews hear the story of the Paxtons, who died seventy years earlier and whose house was torn down shortly thereafter. There was a scandal involving the death of their grown daughter, who had decided to marry against her father's wishes, and it was believed that he had taken his own life two years later and another young woman disappeared in the area more recently. Although the creepy atmosphere is well developed, the lack of a more detailed explanation of what happened to cause the recurring appearance of the house detracts from the story's effectiveness.

The two gentlemen in the title of "Mr. Kershaw and Mr. Wilcox" are neighbors and occasional business associates. Their latest joint venture is promising but expensive and through a technicality, Wilcox plans to seize complete control of the business and leave Kershaw bankrupt. That evening, Kershaw becomes so enraged that he sneaks into Wilcox's house and strangles the man. The next morning he wakens to a message requesting that he call on his neighbor. He is confused but decides to play innocent. To his utter surprise, Wilcox is alive and immediately pledges to renew their agreement after all. It is only then that the two men realize that the murder was all a dream, but that it had been experienced by both of them.

"In the Woods" is more portrait than story. A lonely young woman becomes obsessed with the forest nearby, which seems to her to generate a kind of companionship. "The Late Earl of D" is a very traditional story in which a man experiences a vision of the death of a rich man – supposedly of natural causes although he was actually murdered by his younger brother. A vision is not admissible in a court of law so there is nothing he can do to alter the situation, but the murderer himself dies in an accident only a few days later.

The subject of "Mr. Mortimer's Diary" is an amateur historian who was noted for his discovery of Etruscan artifacts and his writings on the subject. Although at one point another man claimed that Mortimer had stolen the artifacts from him, there was no way to prove this either way and the evidence suggested otherwise. Shortly before his death, Mortimer began to act erratically, sometimes as though he were aware of another party in the room invisible to everyone else. One morning he is found dead in his rooms, having strangled himself.

The rest of the story consists of excerpts from the dead man's diary. Mortimer admits that he defrauded the other man, Bradshaw, but begins to hear his voice and later catch glimpses of him even when he is clearly alone, and he discovers that Bradshaw died a few days earlier. He is clearly being haunted but the closing pages are almost redundant since we already know that he killed himself, presumably at the instigation of Bradshaw's ghost.

There is a benevolent ghost in "The House in the Wood." Two travelers are forced to take shelter in the house of an unscrupulous couple who drug them preparatory to robbery and perhaps murder, but the ghost of the recently deceased daughter of one of them appears and rouses them in the nick of time. "The Steps" is an example of the haunted person story. A soldier is killed in action after being emphatically rejected as a suitor for a young lady, who then begins hearing his footsteps approaching her at odd moments even though no one is visible. Haunting by sound, or clairaudience, is relatively rare in ghost stories.

An artist is commissioned to paint a portrait in "The Young Lady in Black," based only on a brief sketch and an old photograph. For reasons she refuses to explain, the subject is unable to do a formal sitting, but she stresses that she needs the painting quickly and urgently. Some months later he attends a dinner party where he sees her again, but to his consternation he learns afterward that she was invisible to everyone else in the room. Eventually he discovers that she was a ghost who wanted the portrait so that her family would remember her. The story is slightly unusual in that this ghost is visible to others when she needs to be and is capable of paying a substantial sum to the artist as well as moving other physical objects.

"The Downs" is quite minor. A student walking across a stretch of lonely country at night encounters and converses with another man, who turns out to be a ghost. In "The Late Mrs. Fowke" a curate is puzzled by his wife's occasional night long excursions to a remote moor following a period in which she burns odd herbs and sings in a foreign language. He finally decides to follow her and in due course witnesses the convening of some kind of coven who summon an indistinctly shaped form that radiates evil. That evening the creature comes to his wife and she dies in bed. The ending in this instance is very unsatisfactory since it provides no hint of why the evil entity should suddenly turn upon the woman who worshipped it.

"The Picture" is another story whose ending does not measure up. A young woman disappears shortly after having a vision of an older man who is believed to be dead. Her skeleton is later found in a hidden room in the castle at the feet of another, the long dead aristocrat who himself disappeared mysteriously. "Mr. Oliver

Carmichael" is something of a recluse. Following a succession of unpleasant dreams, he meets a young woman in a shop who impresses him as having an evil aspect. The dreams recur in even greater detail, leaving him distressed and unrested. After trying to shrug off the entire sequence of events, he is driven to confront her and explain his problem, but she hints that he is essentially making a pass at her. Months pass in which he dreams of her every night. His eventual salvation is that the blending of their two natures has worked in both directions and some of his goodness has affected her, enough so that she releases him from her magical bondage.

Northcote's longest piece of fiction was "The Governess's Story." A young governess takes a position working for a woman she judges to be rather cool to all the world except her children. The protagonist is almost immediately puzzled by strange sounds at night, as though someone walked through a room that does not appear to exist. She does, however, learn that a family member died years earlier under tragic circumstances. She concludes that during their childhood, her employer treated another child callously and caused him to throw himself from a window.

Although most of these stories are reasonably entertaining, they rarely vary from the formula of the traditional ghost story. In almost every case they are presented with a wealth of immaterial background information that contributes little or nothing to the actual plot. His ghosts are rarely frightening and even more rarely do they do any harm to the living. They are more likely to be tragic or mysterious or in some cases almost inconsequential. His characters are particularly prone to presenting long lists of their credentials, and many of them are able to read such complex emotions into casual glances at the faces of their companions that it is sometimes comical. At his best, he was mediocre and he never seemed interested in treading on unfamiliar territory.

WILLIAM FRYER HARVEY

William Fryer Harvey (1885-1937) was an English Quaker who studied medicine but never actually took up a practice, in part due to his own ill health. He eventually did medical work during World War I, but his health suffered more damage and efforts to work in the field of education later were truncated. He published fifteen books in his life time, many of them collections of short stories, primarily horror and suspense.

His most famous story was "The Beast with Five Fingers" which was filmed in 1946 starring Robert Alda and Peter Lorre. Adrian Borlsover is a mildly eccentric man who loses his sight at the age of fifty. His sensitivity to touch, however, is so acute that he is largely able to function as before, identifying flowers with his hands and carrying on his correspondence as before in his own writing. His nephew, Eustace Borlsover, is a reclusive naturalist who rarely visited his invalid uncle.

As Adrian grows older, Eustace discovers that his uncle has developed the power of automatic writing – his left hand frequently inscribes words while his mind is engaged in another pursuit entirely. On one occasion while his uncle is asleep, Eustace carries on a direct conversation with some entity which is speaking through the automatic writing. There is a hint of evil intimacy that he finds mildly disturbing.

Shortly after the death of Adrian, Eustace receives a package that apparently contains a live animal. Before he can open the package, the creature escapes and conceals itself in his library. He then receives correspondence from his uncle's lawyer indicating that the body had been embalmed but – according to Adrian's last minute instructions – one hand had been severed and mailed to him. Even as he is reading this letter, the mysterious "animal" begins playing with the lights and knocking books from the shelves.

With the aid of a friend, Eustace captures the hand after considerable effort. It seems to have become inanimate again and they secure it – or so they believe – inside its original box before setting out on a brief vacation. A few days later they receive a letter from their housekeeper giving notice because of a strange animal loose in the house. They return and learn that the butler received a note, supposedly from Eustace, telling him to unlock the box holding the hand. Although he didn't see what was inside, it escaped while he was carrying out those instructions.

They eventually capture it, nail it to a board, and lock it in a safe. Unfortunately, burglars break into the house a few months later and the safe is found empty in the morning. Eustace flees to the city but the hand shows up almost immediately and evades capture. Ultimately it causes Eustace's death when, while attempting to prevent entry through the chimney, Eustace starts a fire from which he fails to escape.

As is the case with many supernatural stories from this era, it features protagonists who never appeal to a greater authority to help them evade their doom, even when they have direct evidence to corroborate their story. Although this detracts from the story's realism, it also creates a kind of claustrophobic shell that is very effective in developing atmosphere. This story was quite obviously the inspiration for Marc Brandel's 1979 novel *The Lizard's Tail*, which was filmed as *The Hand*. Animated hands with an independent life have also appeared in the Evil Dead movies and elsewhere.

"Midnight House" is a remote inn visited by the narrator while on a walking tour. At first he is refused entry because the owners insist they are too busy to deal with guests, and the building is in disrepair and shows no signs of actual use as a lodging place. He appeals to the woman in charge pleading the lateness of the hour and the inclement weather and she finally relents. He has nightmares during the night and in the morning discovers that a baby was born in the building during the night, but died before daylight. The story is not overtly supernatural but the narrator suggests that the inn was by its very nature evil.

"The Dabblers" also skirts around the edges of the supernatural. A secret society of boys at a particular school indulges in clandestine singing and chanting one night per year, and it turns out this is a holdover from when the building housed a monastery whose bunks were interested in occult subjects. The story contains an interesting side premise that some traditions are passed from young boys to other young boys, but that these are forgotten by everyone as they turn into adults.

"Unwinding" is a very short mystery story in which a game of memory association leads to the discovery of a murderer. "Mrs. Ormerod" concerns a horrible housekeeper who quietly terrorizes her employers and is presumed to have sent her adopted son to step in front of a car so that he will be too injured to move for months, thus avoiding her being fired. Another murder plot misfires in "Double Demon."

The narrator of "The Tool" is on a walking tour across a moor when he finds the body of a man who appears to have been bludgeoned to death several days earlier. He immediately goes to a nearby village to report his find and discovers that he has somehow lost an entire day. That night he begins to wonder if he killed the man during his blackout, so in the morning he retraces his steps rather than go to the police. This time there is no body and he convinces himself that he imagined the entire thing. But then he discovers that he has missed another day, during which he borrowed a small shovel, and that suggests that he moved and/or buried the body. He tells his story to the police, is tried and committed as criminally insane. He doesn't resent the sentence but concludes that the man was destined to die, and he was simply chosen as the tool to ensure that the death took place. This is an exceptionally good story.

"The Heart of the Fire" is a bit of psychological suspense about a man who commits a murder and discovers that it overshadows the rest of his life. "The Clock" is one of the most subtle supernatural stories of all time. The narrator is asked to stop by a deserted cottage and pick up a clock, but when he arrives, it has been freshly wound even though the building has been securely locked for weeks. The protagonist of "Peter Levisham" is compelled by some unknown force to warn a stranger of danger on three separate occasions..

Andrew Saxon of "Miss Cornelius" is a well respected science teacher who is asked to help investigate what appears to be poltergeist phenomena at the house owned by a bank clerk. There are rappings and things flying about on the very first night and while Saxon cannot explain them all, he is sure that Miss Cornelius – a friend of the beleaguered family – was responsible for some of them. He confronts her, but of course she denies everything. She later suggests that she may have become infected by the real poltergeist.

Saxon is disinclined to believe that, but similar incidents began to occur in his own home and he once sees his wife create one, apparently unaware of what she is doing. But at the end we realize that he is the source of the strange occurrences himself, although there is a somewhat ambiguous ending.

"The Man Who Hated Aspidistras" is a vignette about a man who is raised among those flowers and learns to hate them, but eventually comes to resemble them both physically and in his habits. "Sambo" is a mild variation of the demonic doll story, with an African effigy actually representing a god and forcing its young owner to set aside her other dolls. "The Star" is a rather pointless vignette about a man criticizing a sermon. "Across the Moors" is another vignette, this one about an encounter with a friendly ghost by a woman walking on the moor at night.

"The Follower" is an odd little tale in which a writer imagines that two reclusive men are actually deciphering ancient texts, but when he meets them, they announce that they are doing exactly that and they hope he will keep their confidence, a clear indication that they know he had planned to write a story using that plot. "August Heat", one of his best known stories, has a somewhat similar theme. An artist impulsively draws the portrait of a man being sentenced in a court room. He then goes for a walk and finds that very same man working a shop that carves tombstones. The one he is working on – intended for an exhibition – bears the artist's name. They decide that for safety's sake he should stay with the craftsman until the day of his forecast death ends, and the story concludes with the man sharpening his chisel.

"Sarah Bennett's Possession" is a somewhat disorganized story about a woman who is unconsciously channeling messages from her dead husband. "Miss Avenal" is an excellent story about a woman who agrees to be a kind of nurse and companion to a woman who seems weak and confused, only to eventually learn that the woman is taking away her own life and enthusiasm to restore her own youth.

"The Ankardine Pew" is more complex. Two gentlemen are considering taking rooms rented by the elderly Miss Ankardyne, who seems a peaceful, friendly person despite the fact that almost every animal shares a deep seated antipathy toward her. One of the two – the first of two narrators – is already staying there while repairs and alterations are underway in anticipation of their formally moving in. Miss Ankardyne believes the house to be haunted but believes that the spirits involved are now mostly at rest.

The haunting – which the first of the two men confirms – involves the cry of birds in the night, perhaps owls, and visual hallucinations of bright lights, sometimes accompanied by a sharp pain in the tongue. The occurrences are most frequent in Miss Ankardyne's bedroom but are not confined to a single location. The second man sleeps in the house and has a vision connected to an engraving in the disused church that adjoins the house. The inscription refers to the use of birds to cleanse a house of evil and was the epitaph for another Ankardyne who died a century earlier. Months later, he discovers a reference to this gentleman having conducted a cock fight in the empty church, after which he tortured one of the birds to death.

"Last of the Race" sets up an interesting situation but the ending miscarries. A scientist determined to make up for a life filled with failures tracks down the last representative of a race of flightless birds unknown to science. Unfortunately, he finds himself trapped on the island after he captures the bird, and the stories ends as he slowly succumbs to a fever. "Deaf and Dumb" describes the foreshortened career of a games keeper when he is compelled to enforce anti-poaching laws.

"A Middle-Class Tragedy" is a clever but non-fantastic story in which a man decides to take advantage of a disastrous accident to fake his own death and disappear from an unhappy marriage, only to reconsider and return home to find that his wife had gone away on her own and never knew he was absent. The protagonist of "The Fern" knows of a rare plant and hopes to buy the land where it grows, only to discover at the last moment that someone has casually destroyed it.

"The Angel of Stone" is a vignette about a man who finds a hundred year old note tucked inside a church statue. "The Tortoise" is a somewhat convoluted tale of murder and "After the Flower Show" is a commentary on human competitiveness. "The Desecrator" involves a mysterious defacement of a monument, but the resolution is mundane.

In fact most of Harvey's remaining short fiction consists of unremarkable crime stories, a few of which are mildly clever. "Dead of Night" is not supernatural, but it is a very atmospheric story of a man injured in an accident during an air raid and power failure. He is inadvertently sent to the morgue instead of a treatment room. "The

Habeas Corpus Club" is an amusing fantasy at which all of the murdered characters from mystery novels – who have died before their characters could be developed – form a club where they rent themselves out over and over again for new novels. Harvey was a consistently skillful writer but other than a handful of exceptional stories, his output was rather routine.

MRS. J.H. RIDDELL

Charlotte Eliza Dawson Cowan (1832-1906) was born in Ireland and moved to London where she married Joseph Hadley Riddell in 1857. Riddell suffered a severe financial setback and his wife began to write to pay the bills. He died in 1880 and she struggled to make ends meet for the rest of her life despite her popularity as a writer. She was also part owner of a literary magazine. Riddell wrote more than fifty novels of which at least five contained supernatural elements, but she is best known for her shorter ghost stories, which were noted for the depth of her characterizations.

Riddell's two best known stories are probably "Nut Bush Farm" and "The Open Door." The first of these is very conventional. A man facing a long recuperation from an illness purchases a small country farm. Shortly after moving in, he hears rumors that a path nearby is haunted. His sister reports seeing the ghost during the daylight, but he is convinced she was mistaken. That night, he ventures out himself and encounters what he believes to be the ghost of the previous tenant of the farm, who is believed to have run off with a young girl and all of his savings. He believes that the man was actually murdered for the money, and the girl in question turns up working in another village, completely unaware of her supposed elopement. He identifies a neighbor as the murderer, recovers the money for the widow, and finds the body concealed in the overgrowth.

"The Open Door" is a nicely constructed haunted house story. An ambitious young clerk volunteers to spend two weeks in an empty house where one of the doors refuses to stay shut. The door leads to a room where an unsolved murder was committed and the legend is that the door will not remain shut until the killer is identified. Our hero quickly concludes that the door is indeed being opened by a supernatural force, but he also notices that his rifle has been tampered with and his possessions have been gone through, suggesting there is a human agency involved as well. He eventually surprises the murderer, a woman who stood to inherit a substantial fortune unless a missing will was located, and survives when she shoots him. The ending is slightly clumsy but not fatally so.

The protagonist of "The Banshee's Warning" (aka "Hertford O'Donnell's Warning") is Hertford O'Donnell, a skilled physician working in the era before chloroform was in use. Although he has many positive attributes, he is also a very hard man who views his patients as objects to be repaired rather than as actual people. Although fairly popular with most of the patients he treats because of his skills, O'Donnell is viewed with suspicion because of his Irish lineage.

Resigned to the fact that he will never progress very far in his profession, O'Donnell decides that he needs to marry a rich heiress to provide for his declining years. To this end, he begins to court an elderly unmarried woman, but upon doing so he hears briefly a strange wailing in his apartment. He recognizes it as the cry of a banshee, foretelling death. Later that night he awakens with the conviction that he needs to go to the hospital. He does so and learns that someone was just sent to summon him because of a severely injured child requiring an amputation. While preparing, he sees the figure of a woman who is invisible to everyone else except the injured boy. The boy dies and afterward O'Donnell discovers that the boy was his own son, conceived during his youth in a love affair that was ended by family strife. The story is effective, though somewhat longwinded and prone to interludes of philosophy.

"The Last of Squire Ennismore" is a very short tale of a mysterious figure who walks the beach near the site of a shipwreck and who apparently lures a local man of ill repute to his doom. "A Strange Christmas Game" opens with John Lester inheriting the much diminished family estate from an uncle he never met. The house has been closed up for many years and inevitably there are stories of ghosts connected to the disappearance of another relative decades earlier. There are strange noises leading up to a ghostly reenactment of a duel, which explains the disappearance.

"The Old House in Vauxhall Walk" is rather routine. A homeless man shelters in an empty house only to find that ghostly dramas manifest themselves during the night. "Sandy the Tinker" has an ambiguous ending. A clergyman dreams of an encounter with the devil requiring him to send someone to be sacrificed or to die himself. He chooses a tinker, but ultimately relents at the last moment. The tinker, however, is accidentally killed right on schedule.

"Forewarned, Forearmed" opens with a long character study of a man who then takes over as narrator. He has long experienced a recurring dream of an encounter with an old friend that always ends with a sense of impending doom. When he finds himself actually undergoing a real life version of that dream, he feels a growing sense of panic. He is sure that a complete stranger will attempt to murder his friend, so he watches clandestinely and when the act begins to play out in earnest, he shoots the assailant in the shoulder. Years later, he encounters the man again and confronts him, literally frightening the man to death.

"Walnut-Tree House" is another variation of the missing will. The new owner of an old house is troubled by the specter of a young child until he locates the will of a former owner and restores the legacy to a young girl, the ghost's sister. "Why Doctor Cray Left Southam" is more mystery than supernatural. A doctor suspects that one of his patients is being slowly poisoned by her husband following what appears to have been a precognitive dream. He foils the plot but the woman refuses to believe him and goes back to her husband.

A well liked man named Richard Tippens purchases an old house in "Old Mrs. Jones." Although there are rumors that it is haunted by Mrs. Jones, who disappeared and reportedly will not rest until she is properly buried, Tippens and his wife initially see nothing to suggest the stories are true. Then one of the servants faints after encountering the image of the woman and others begin to see her at odd moments and with increasing frequency.

Tippens and his wife investigate and find out that Doctor Jones and his wife, the previous tenants, both disappeared under questionable circumstances and that the local people believe he murdered her and then absconded. Eventually they abandon the house and shortly afterward it is burned to the ground, apparently by the figure of an unidentified woman. We are left to speculate about whether or not Mrs. Jones was a witch.

"Conn Kilrea" concerns a taciturn soldier who sees the ghost of an ancestor who appears to each member of his family just before they die. His attempt to seek an explanation from a clergyman is rebuffed because the latter does not believe that the dead return to the world. Eventually he realizes that it was not his death that was being foretold. "A Terrible Vengeance" tells the story of a murderer who is followed by the damp footsteps of the woman he drowned.

"'Diarmid Chittock's Story" opens with the discovery by Cyril Danson that he has no interest in the modern world and wishes to travel to unexplored or at least unfamiliar lands, particularly as he has been recently jilted. He is forced to settle for a prolonged stay at the empty castle of his friend, Diarmid Chittock, who prefers to live in London. He is not there long before he hears the story of a local man who disappeared inexplicably one night. Danson becomes interested in the missing man's daughter, Oona, and begins asking questions about the disappearance. He discovers that Oona refused the advances of his friend Diarmid and decides to try to kindle a romance at second hand. Predictably he hears strange sounds at night. In due course he finds the body and the killer, Chittock, commits suicide. This one is a bit long winded but the story is quite nicely constructed.

Riddell's novels follow the same pattern as her short fiction but it is worthwhile examining some of them. The narrator of *The Haunted House at Latchford* (1872, aka *Fairy Water*) is a lawyer turned writer named H. Stafford Trevor. The opening provides some rambling background on the narrator and describes Fairy Water, a cottage of which he is fond. Fairy Water is owned by Captain Geoffrey Trevor, a retired seaman, who late in life announces his engagement to Mary Ashley.

There is considerable mystery about the marriage. Ashley is clearly heartbroken at the prospect, and there seems to be no good reason why the captain would marry a penniless younger woman with no prospects. As the years pass, he becomes increasingly obsessed with her, ignoring his own children, jealously preventing her from having any life of her own.

Ten years later he dies and the will proves burdensome. Mary is given an income and use of the property until her oldest child reaches his majority, but if she should ever remarry, she immediately loses everything, including custody of her own children. She is resigned to a life of perpetual widowhood, with the narrator as her only close friend.

Trevor decides to settle down and rents a house of his own, but whenever he sleeps there he has the feeling that he is not alone in his own chambers. His servant tells him that the house has a reputation of being haunted and that the previous resident left in a rush after some unspecified event. He convinces the servant to tell him the story, which involves a murder and the disappearance of a woman who was known to be in possession of valuable jewelry. Ever since then, people have reported feeling a presence in the house, though no one has ever actually seen a ghost.

Trevor suspects that the housekeeper may be trying to drive him away so that she can resume her tenure as caretaker without having to answer to anyone else. Nevertheless, he continues to sense that he is not alone. Despite his reservations, he hopes to purchase the property outright. The ghost then begins to appear in dreams, clearly a woman and probably the spirit of the one who disappeared. Meanwhile, a descendant of the presumed murderer named Waldrum has been helping deal with some physical problems afflicting the oldest of Mary's children and she is somewhat melancholy because all of her children seem so captivated by him.

Trevor decides to tear down the old part of the house in order to lay the ghost. The workers find a secret passage with bones and a large cache of jewels. Trevor gives the jewels to Waldrum, who is in love with the widow, so that they can afford to lose her inheritance, but then by chance a new, unsuspected will is found that allows her to remarry. Everyone lives happily ever after in this relatively low key ghost story.

In *The Uninhabited House* (1875), the narrator is the lawyer for Mrs. Blake, who wishes to rent out a house that her niece owns and which has a bad reputation. One tenant after another has complained and moved away and it is often vacant for extended periods of time. A significant portion of the first half of the novel consists of a history of the family, which has no supernatural content and is only of moderate interest, although it does set up the conditions for the haunting.

Eventually it is concluded that something is wrong, although the lawyers suspect a living person is at fault rather than a ghost. The protagonist is sent to investigate, but he is skeptical of the various reports he hears about things being moved by unseen hands and strange noises in the night. At this point there is a lengthy digression into the life story of the protagonist, which might easily have been left out entirely.

He ultimately decides to stay at the house himself and on the very first night he experiences the strange sounds reported by previous tenants. A ghost then appears, leads him to the nearby graveyard, and then disappears after leaving a cryptic message. The next day the protagonist has the distinct feeling that he is being watched, a sensation which continues unabated in the days that follow. In due course, he solves the mystery of an earlier death and that clears the atmosphere in the house. This was essentially a longer version of the same story she had told at shorter length on several previous occasions.

The Haunted River (1877) opens with two sisters initiating a search for a cottage in which to live. They find a place near an abandoned mill set beside a river. They agree to rent it although one of the sisters, the narrator, experiences unsettling feelings when she goes inside. They learn that the mill was owned by a man named Dingley, who mysteriously drowned, perhaps a suicide. They also hear of a ghostly figure who reportedly was seen near the mill some years later.

One day the sister is painting a picture of the mill when she sees a man in the distance, his posture suggesting despondency. She adds him to the painting without knowing who he is. When she tries to approach him, however, he suddenly disappears. Both sisters suspect that their landlord has cheated them by putting a provision in the lease agreement that requires additional payments they had not expected.

Their landlord, who has been making unwanted overtures of a romantic nature, recognizes the figure in the painting as Dingley. The artist sees him in her dreams and occasionally, from a distance, while awake. The sisters have also befriend a local woman, reputed to be a witch, and they slowly begin to realize that the landlord cheated Dingley just as he did they themselves, and that Dingley cannot rest in his grave. There is considerably more supernatural content to this than to Riddell's other novels, some of it mildly eerie, though it is tame by contemporary standards.

The Disappearance of Jeremiah Redworth (1878) opens with the title character announcing that he is walking to a nearby village and returning late, but he never arrives back at home. His family discovers that he met a neighbor on his way back who reports that Redworth was in a very bad mood at the time. His path would have taken him past Taunton Hall, whose current owner has an unsavory reputation.

His family launches a search and discovers that he took out a large amount of cash during his trip. This suggests that he might have been robbed. The people at Taunton Hall deny that he stopped there. The police suspect his son John may have done away with his father in anticipation of his share of the estate, but they have no evidence and no body.

Taunton Hall has a reputation for being haunted although there have been no incidents in more than a generation. Redworth's niece pays a visit and has a brief glimpse of her uncle's apparition, which promptly fades away. There are a few more mild bits of ghostly interference before the mystery is solved. Quite short and very low key.

The Nun's Curse (1888) was her next to final novel. It opens with the people of Donegal quietly pleased that Duke Conway, a cruel and repressive man, has finally died. His will leaves everything to his godson, Marmaduke Conway, leaving his nephew Terence, who was expected to be a major beneficiary, virtually destitute. Terence is traveling one day when he meets one of the local people who disparages the dead man and insists the family and its holding are under the nun's curse, although he does not know the details.

Terence has inherited the family home, but without any money to maintain it, and he unwisely borrowed large sums in expectation of his inheritance. The loyal family servant, Ann Patterson, urges him to sell the estate – which would break the curse – but he is reluctant to part with it. An acquaintance, Philippa Dutton, also urges him to retain the property. Others have ambivalent positions because it is not clear to them that selling the property will lift the curse, or because they don't believe in the curse in the first place.

A local clergyman, Mr. McKye, explains the origin of the curse to Terence. Sister Agnes was the sole survivor when a neighbor and his followers attacked the local convent and killed everyone else. Terence's ancestor happened to encounter the woman and set his dogs on her and although they didn't kill her, she died the following day after telling him that his family was cursed and would never be happy or successful so long as they lived on the family estate. The curse has been in effect for three centuries.

Unfortunately the bulk of the novel is a tedious series of incidents involving two primary themes. The first is Terence's interest in marrying Philippa, who seems oddly reluctant to commit herself despite her supposed interest in the maintenance of the Conway estate. The second consists of Terence's efforts to find a way to maintain the estate in a solvent condition. Although he intends to treat his tenants honorably, the lack of funds available to him results in pressure to raise rents and commit other acts which detract from his popularity with the local people.

Terence eventually convinces Philippa to marry him, but his fortunes take a turn for the worse before their wedding. The curse seems to have taken effect despite his skepticism. Philippa keeps moving the wedding date further off and an old girlfriend troubles Terence's conscience. His tenants become restive and his own personality coarsens. The scandal erupts into the open and the wedding is canceled. He is forced by circumstances to marry the girlfriend, Grace, who is pregnant, and is then shot from ambush and nearly dies.

His fortunes have improved somewhat as the book ends, but there are hints that his son has an evil streak and that the nun's curse is still in force. Although we are to believe that the curse is real, there is little direct evidence of it, and none of the melodramatic appearances of a shrouded figure that one might expect with a plot of this sort. Riddell's characterization is as deft as ever and the plot is reasonably lively, but there is little if any suspense and the supernatural element is almost invisible.

Riddell's work is noteworthy in large part because of the depth of her characterization. It is unfortunate that her supernatural fiction rarely veered away from its standard formula, and this is perhaps a function of her need to produce a great deal of work to pay her bills. She did introduce some minor variations and some of the imagery is quite striking, but no single story was remarkable enough to establish her reputation.

MARJORIE BOWEN/ JOSEPH SHEARING

Both Marjorie Bowen and Joseph Shearing were pseudonyms by Gabrielle Margaret Long (1995-1952), born into a poor family which she more or less supported with her writing from the time she turned eighteen onward. Author off about 150 books under a variety of names, she was particularly successful writing historical fiction, although she is just as well remembered today for her short supernatural stories. Several of her novels also featured supernatural events.

The two most successful of her weird novels were *Black Magic* (1909), which was probably the second novel she wrote and which appeared as by Marjorie Bowen, and *The Fetch* (aka *The Spectral Bride*) which was published in 1942, quite late in her career and under the name Joseph Shearing. The first was reprinted as part of Dennis Wheatley's "Library of the Occult."

Black Magic – whose subtitle is "the rise and fall of the anti-Christ" - opens with a young man named Dirk Renswoude applying the finishing touches to a statue of the devil in his private apartment some time during the Middle Ages. He is visited by Balthasar of Coutrai, who was married against his will to an heiress who was living in a convent at the time and who, with the aid of her fellow nuns, faked her own death to avoid consummating the marriage. Years later she changes her mind and appeals to her husband to rescue her from the convent, but he fails to respond. A war destroys the convent and she takes shelter with Renswoude until her real death some time later.

Balthasar's friend Thierry is a scholar of sorts and he and Renswoude share their disdain for the church and an interest in black magic. The two men decide to summon an evil spirit and demand that it reveal the future, and their first attempt to do so is somewhat successful, although the spell is broken before they can learn much. It is strongly implied that the two men are attracted to each other but naturally such things could not be explicitly described in 1909.

The two men decide to travel to Basle, a seat of much arcane learning. During their journey, they see a fantastic figure striding across the sky. They reach Basle and study there for almost a year before trouble starts up. Their friendship is strained when Theirry meets and speaks well of Jacobea, a young woman who is the ward of the emperor. Dirk is unpopular and has a confrontation with another student, Joris, whom he strikes down with a magical illness. Unfortunately, he is the obvious suspect and a mob invades his room, discovers his forbidden magical implements, and attacks him. Theirry helps him to escape and run away. Up until this point, Dirk has been the dominant member of the pair, but now he seems disoriented and ineffectual.

The two take shelter at a nearby estate which, they learn, is the temporary residence of Jacobea. Dirk regains the initiative and Theirry, who has begun to have doubts about the wisdom of pursuing the dark arts, grows increasingly uneasy. Nevertheless he is tantalized by the idea of using a spell to win the love of Jacobea. Dirk, however, does not want to lose his companion and instead suggests to the steward, Sebastian, that he might win the heart of his mistress – even though Sebastian is already married.

The twosome departs after a night's stay and meet a monk named Saint Ambrose on their way to Frankfort. He is carrying a great deal of gold with him which they steal after subduing him and travel on to Frankfort. Their success has erased Theirry's doubts about committing himself to the devil. They take lodgings with Nathalie, who is reputed to be a witch.

Theirry has not forgotten Jacobea, however, and eventually goes to see her, much to the dismay of Dirk. Nathalie tries to convince him that he is better off without Theirry, but Dirk is determined to have him back, although he believes that Jacobea will herself eventually drive him away without any need for magical intervention.

Dirk is approached by another woman, Ysabeau, who knows about his past and tells him that Joris died. She wants his assistance in striking back at the man she hates, whom she does not name. Dirk consults a demonic entity who identifies her. She is the wife of the current emperor and the man she wants destroyed is her husband so that she can marry her lover, Balthasar of Coutrai. Balthasar, however, is loyal to the emperor, Melchoir.

Dirk, now using the name Constantine, visits the empress shortly after she has a violent quarrel with her husband, who is less ambitious politically than she is. Dirk and Nathalie bewitch Jacobea's horse so that she is lost in a forest where they can meet with her unobserved. Dirk tries to force her to admit her love for Sebastian and suggests that she might arrange the death of his wife so that they could be together. He also attempts reconciliation with Theirry, who sees an inhuman figure in Dirk's chambers and is horrified despite his previous experience of otherworldly creatures.

Theirry and Jacobea are now united by their fear and loathing of Dirk, although both still feel the appeal of his power. Theirry tells Dirk that their friendship is at an end. Dirk then provides Ysabeau with a magical potion that allows her to poison and kill the emperor, but some of the nobles are convinced that she was responsible and threaten to hold her to account for his death.

Dirk tells Jacobea that she could be free to marry Sebastian if his wife died, and that he would be happy to provide the means for her to suffer the same fate as the emperor. She resists, but Sebastian is more pliable and Jacobea fails to dissuade him from leaving on a mission of murder. Theirry has promised to return to Dirk if Jacobea proves capable of evil, and through Dirk's manipulations even Sebastian believes that she herself commanded him to kill his wife.

Nathalie predicts that Theirry will be the cause of Dirk's doom but he ignores her. Balthasar marries Ysabeau and is chosen to be the next emperor. Ysabeau has accused Hugo of Rooselaare of treason and ordered him executed, but Dirk becomes quite upset and insists that she should pardon him, although he will not explain himself. Hugo was foremost among those who accused Ysabeau of murder. She reluctantly issues the pardon but Hugo is executed before Dirk can deliver it.

Theirry abandons him again and the empress raises the people against Dirk and Nathalie. A messenger from Hell warns Dirk to flee just in time to escape death. He is in dire straits when he runs into Saint Ambrose. He convinces the monk he has repented of his sins while still communing with the messenger from Hell. Together they travel to Paris and beyond.

Several years later Theirry goes to Rome, hoping to confess his sins to a high official of the church. He is received by Cardinal Caprarola, reputedly the worthiest of all the cardinals, but to his utter horror he recognizes the man as Dirk Renswoude. Dirk is next in line to be Pope, despite the opposition of Ysabeau, who knows his true identity. He attempts to neutralize her by threatening to reveal that Balthasar's first wife, Ursula, is not dead after all and that therefore her own marriage is invalid.

Theirry is at his wit's end when he is accosted by a masked dancer who tells him that it is possible that he might become the next emperor. He accuses her of witchcraft but she denies the charge. He is still trying to decide what course of action to take when Dirk is proclaimed Pope, taking the name Michael II. He summons Balthasar and demands that he set aside Ysabeau, revealing to him that Ursula is still alive. Ursula, unsurprisingly, is the mysterious dancer who spoke to Theirry. Theirry is reunited with Jacobea, who never married Sebastian and is worn down with guilt about the death of his wife.

The Pope and the Emperor are at war. Theirry leads the Pope's army and Balthasar is defeated, despite Ysabeau's attempt to sacrifice herself to save her husband by admitting that she killed Melchoir. Dirk excommunicates her and has her cast out of the city. Theirry is to be proclaimed emperor of Germany. For the final time, he abandons Dirk and reveals all in a public denouncement that leads to a general rebellion against the new Pope. Faced with defeat, Dirk takes his own life just before the Vatican is conquered. Dirk is in fact Ursula, who has been posing as a man.

This is a lengthy, involved, and generally lively novel which might have remained popular if the supernatural element had been stronger. The reader might be understandably impatient with Theirry, who dithers and wrings his hands constantly, changes sides frequently, and who never develops into a sympathetic character. Dirk is the best drawn of the characters, but we rarely see any of his inner thoughts and his drive toward evil is never explained.

Long's second significant novel of the supernatural was *The Spectral Bride* (aka *The Fetch*), which appeared under the name Joseph Shearing. Set in the 1870s, it opens with a glimpse of the Fenton household. Sisters Caroline and Adelaide are both looking for a likely husband of comfortable means. Their father is an invalid and they are living primarily on his pension. The family is in the limbo between classes, unable to find a place among the aristocrats but a bit too affected to fit in with those in their own income level.

Adelaide insists that she has a rich beau named Basil whom she meets secretly in the woods, and she is supported by her sister. Her mother, however, has doubts because she can find no independent confirmation that Basil even exists. "Basil" appears to be the false name of James Daintry, Lord Manton, son of a wealthy nobleman and only a few months short of his birthday, at which time he will become independently wealthy in his own right. His grandfather the Earl is somewhat concerned that Daintry may be brooding about the death of an ancestor by hanging following his conviction for murder. The dead man's victim has a legend connected to her and is known as the Spectral Bride. Her name was Harriet Bond and she was employed as a servant at the local inn.

In fact Daintry is convinced that he has encountered the ghost (or fetch) of the dead woman and that she wants revenge against the descendant of the man who killed her. He has been investigating the circumstances surrounding her death, despite efforts by his family to expunge the event from the memories of the local residents. He has found a painting of Bond and she bears a strong resemblance to Adelaide Fenton, whom he has been secretly meeting in the woods.

Daintry consults with Lucas Perry, who has a reputation for his knowledge of occult events. His grandfather clearly disapproves of Perry and considers sending Daintry abroad to get him away from the village. The Earl has a close friend who discovers that Daintry has been seeing Adelaide and he puts pressure on her mother to send her away or face pressure to move the entire family.

Bond speaks to Daintry during a séance which appears to be genuine. He also finds an old letter that describes another man's encounter with Bond's ghost years earlier. As a small crisis approaches, the situation changes dramatically and it appears that Adelaide may be truly engaged to be married – but not to Daintry. The reader will be startled at this point when "Basil" identifies himself as another aristocrat named Seagrove rather than Daintry, despite all the parallels between their two situations. His grandfather, also an earl, has recently died.

The sister gets involved and it becomes obvious that Seagrove is mentally disturbed. The climax comes when he arranges to meet her in secret at a mausoleum, and he succumbs to madness and kills her. Despite the melodramatic ending, the story is tedious and the payoff is not nearly adequate given the long buildup.

The short horror stories were almost all published under the Bowen byline and many of them are now hard to find. The large number of collections attributed to her is misleading, however, as they often share stories from other volumes. Although none of these were outstanding classics of the genre, they are typically well written, imaginative, and suspenseful and it is worth looking at some of them.

"The Fair Hair of Ambrosine" reflects Bowen's interest in historical settings as this one is set during the French Revolution. Claude Boucher is a minor official in the revolutionary government who is trying to keep a low profile because of recent internal purges. He was romantically involved with an actress who was found murdered in her home, apparently the victim of a burglar. Boucher has had troubling dreams in which he accompanies a sinister man whose face he does not see but whom he believes to be his lover's killer until the latter turns and kills him as well. He even knows the date of his dream death – which takes place in the dead woman's empty house - and as it approaches he becomes convinced that he has had a vision of the future. Ultimately he decides to take a friend with him so that he will not have to face his nemesis alone, but naturally the friend turns out to be the killer.

"Crown Derby Plate" is probably the best known of the short stories. A woman once bought a set of China from a neighboring family but one plate was missing. When she learns that the house and all of its contents were sold to someone new, she decides to pay a visit and find out whether they ever found the plate. She is greeted by an odd figure who claims to own the house and who gives her the missing plate, but it is only after she leaves that she discovers that the house is currently empty and that she was talking to the family ghost.

In "The Housekeeper", a dissolute man who murdered his wife discovers that she is still tidying up his house and this revelation drives him to confess. "Elsie's Lonely Afternoon" has no fantastic content, although the young protagonist thinks her uncle is actually a ghost, but the way she is treated by her grandmother – her current guardian – is close to horror.

"Florence Flannery" has a very similar protagonist, recently married to a woman, who attracted him initially because her name is the same as one engraved in the family house, with the date 1500. The legend is that the original Florence betrayed her lover and was cursed to walk the earth until he had his revenge. There is also a broken down sailor in the neighborhood and it is not difficult to predict that he is the thwarted lover, since the two of them both have trouble with their memories. Weird events follow until finally the woman is devoured by the man transformed into a sea creature. This is one of Bowen's best tales.

"The Bishop of Hell" is another historical horror story, set in 1770. An amoral rake has run off with the wife of a married man who vows to challenge him to a duel if he ever returns to England. Through a chain of circumstance, the miscreant inherits a title and eventually faces up to the duel, which results in his having the lower half of his face horribly mutilated. He kills his mistress in a rage after which he takes his own life. His ghost then briefly returns from Hell to visit the narrator.

"The Extraordinary Adventure of Mr. John Proudie" takes place in 1690. It's a rather routine story of ghostly revenge in which a doctor is lured out on a night call that ends with his death. In "The Scoured Silk" the ghost of a man's dead first wife targets his new fiancé with subtle acts of terror connected to a worn silken garment. "The Hidden Ape" is non-fantastic. A scholar discovers that his assistant was once accused of murder and dismisses him, and the assistant then strangles the scholar's ward.

The narrator of "The Avenging of Ann Leete" finds mention of Ann Leete in his new home but no one in the community is able, or willing, to talk about her. He eventually meets an elderly man who was once in love with Leete and announces that she was murdered before they could be married. Her ghost appeared to him and identified the man who murdered her, who died by his own hand some time later. "Ann Mellor's Lover" has a rather similar premise. This time the narrator finds a sketch of a woman in an old book and decides to figure out who she was. He later sees a tombstone and through some clairvoyant ability determines that this is the sketched woman's grave. He then dreams that he is a man named Ericson who planned to abduct Mellor and force her to marry him. He killed her instead and was himself hanged for the crime.

Two dissolute young men take shelter in a poor woman's house in "Kecksies," where they find a man dead who was reputed to be a warlock and who had pursued the wife of one of the two protagonists for a time. They throw the body out into the woods, but it rises, then rapes and murders the woman he coveted in life. This is easily Bowen's most overtly horrifying story.

In "Raw Material" an elderly woman dies under suspicious circumstances, perhaps murdered, perhaps suicide, perhaps felled by an accidental overdose of her medication. Some years earlier she had cleaned out a substantial bank account and no one has any idea where the money has gone. Her niece and nephew both insist that they did not even know of its existence, but some years later the niece has died and the nephew, on his deathbed, admits that they poisoned her for her money. But he also insists that they contacted the dead woman through a medium and that she told them they should have done it sooner because she realized now she had never really enjoyed having either her wealth or her life.

"The Sign-Painter and the Crystal Fishes" is a rather awkward story about a man seeking revenge on those who have wronged him, and who perseveres even after his own death. "The Breakdown" is another story about a mysterious portrait. A traveler takes shelter in a strange inn where supposedly one's wishes can be granted and he wishes to meet the woman whose picture he once cherished. Her ghost appears, although he doesn't realize that she is dead until sometime later.

A student of magic finds a book of powerful ancient magic in a novelty shop in "One Remained Behind." This is one of Bowen's rare excursions into humor as the story becomes a variation of the deal with the devil puzzle. "The House by the Poppy Field" never really resolves its premise. A man inherits a house that seems to him to be waiting for someone and later learns that his predecessor jokingly invited death itself to pay him a visit. "Half-Past Two" involves a man who stole from a companion who subsequently died, but the companion has returned for vengeance.

There are occasional moments of brilliance in some of the short stories, but they rarely last for long and most of the tales are rather pedestrian. Her true interest was in historical fiction and that is certainly where she concentrated her talents. It is ironic that they are largely forgotten while she is still remembered as a horror writer.

RUSSELL KIRK

Russell Kirk (1918-1994) was a noted but unconventional conservative political commentator who supported Norman Thomas and Gene McCarthy at one time or another. His book The *Conservative Mind* was quite influential. His fiction output consisted of twenty two short stories and three novels, but the stories have been collected in various configurations under half a dozen different titles.

"Uncle Isaiah" opens with a laundry business receiving an extortion threat from a local gangster. The owner attempts to find his uncle, missing nearly ten years, who has a reputation for toughness. He hears his uncle's voice from behind a closed door but never sees him and the older man assures him that he will take care of the matter. That night he appears to the gangster and after a brief scuffle, both disappear, never to be seen again. There is a suggestion that he is actually a ghost or revenant rather than a living man, but Kirk never tells us this explicitly.

Kirk's conservative politics show somewhat in "Ex Tenebris." An elderly retired woman insists upon staying in her cottage in a small village that has been otherwise cleared of occupants. A "progressive" politician is impatient to complete the demolition of the town and is prepared to take extraordinary steps to force her to relocate to a planned community. He is a caricature, of course, opposed to religion, tradition, the natural world, and everything else that Kirk feels worth preserving.

One afternoon she is visiting the deconsecrated church when she meets a man who says he is the vicar. In fact, he is the ghost of a long dead clergyman who may have committed murder shortly before his own death. The ghost then calls the politician, arranges a meeting, and when the man refuses to change his stance, the roof of the church porch falls upon him and kills him.

"The Surly Sullen Bell" is Kirk's best known story. It opens with a situation similar to that in "Ex Tenebris." A decaying district near St Louis is being demolished in order to build a park, a development which the omniscient narrator clearly believes is a sin against history and tradition. The protagonist, Frank Loring, admits openly that he is a reactionary.

Loring is a traveling salesman who is surprised to receive an invitation to dinner from Godfrey Schumacher, whose wife Nancy Loring once wooed himself. He finds her ill, suffering from nightmares, and learns that various doctors have failed to discover what is wrong with her. Schumacher brews a special coffee, of which the reader is right to be suspicious, because the following morning Loring falls prey to weakness and pain, which lasts for several days. He eventually realizes on some spiritual level that he is being poisoned and calls the police, but it is too late for Nancy. The title is taken from Shakespeare and is the sound heard when a soul leaves the world of the living.

"The Cellar of Little Egypt" is also quite good. Three men murder a fourth. A local resident is mildly clairvoyant and believes he knows who is responsible, but when he confronts them in the basement of a local bar, they kill him and dispose of the body. His ghost appears during a smoky fire and one man is frightened enough to commit suicide. There is a falling out between the other two and one kills the other, only to be killed himself by the dead man.

In "Sorworth Place" a traveler named Bain becomes interested in a recent widow, Ann Lurlin, and her picturesque home. She has trouble keeping help because they hear voices whispering, and she confesses that she is still afraid of her dead husband, who had himself buried on the grounds of the house, which is now greatly in need of repairs that she cannot afford. Both of them see, or half see, a figure in the distance while they are walking near the house. She fears that her husband will return on the anniversary of his death, and his body does rise. Bain sacrifices himself by grasping the corpse and leaping into the sea. The creepy atmosphere is quite strong in this story.

"Beyond the Stumps" is somewhat disappointing. A persistent census taker presses a rural family to provide the information he requires and discovers that there might be witchcraft behind the family's secretiveness. In "What Shadows We Pursue" a book dealer is clearing out a private library he just purchased from a family that is clearly not right mentally. Murder follows and a ghostly presence foils the killer.

"Off the Sand Road" is a non-fantastic account of a man abused by his wife who commits suicide. Two inept hunters encounter a rural family in "Skyberia" and are told that the holdouts against civilization will survive when society collapses. "Lost Lake" is a supposedly true account of a remote area whose inhabitants, animal or human, invariably die prematurely.

"The Invasion of the Church of the Holy Ghost" is colored with Kirk's political outlook. The narrator is a priest who is appalled by the liberal bent of his superiors. His close friend is Fork Causland, a blind man who refuses to accept welfare and does odd jobs for a living. Causland testified in a murder case but the corrupt courts released the three criminals. They attempt to murder Causland, who manages to kill three of his attackers, thereby acquiring a reputation as someone to be feared.

Two years later, Julie Tilton arrives in town, looking for her brother who turns out to be the dead gangster. They conceal the truth from her but the dead man's spirit possesses the priest, who begins to plan the debasement of Tilton. The priest manages to escape the possession in the nick of time and defeats four malevolent spirits with the aid of an entity whose nature is never quite explained. The climax is rather disappointing as the protagonist's salvation results almost literally by means of a deus ex machina.

"The Peculiar Demesne of Archvicar Gerontion" takes place in an unnamed Muslim nation. It is a story within a story that is revealed after a discussion of ghost stories among people attending a party. Gerontion was the self described head of an independent church, but also a known dealer in dangerous drugs. Through a legal maneuver of dubious validity, he is moved from the local jail to one reserved for English citizens charged with local crimes. There he slowly betrays his confederates but refuses to clear up questions about his own origins. Faced with prison, he gives his captor a drug which causes him to make a mental visit to another reality. This story is spoiled by flowery language and an unclear ending.

"The Reflex-Man in Whinnymuir Close" is cast in the form of an old manuscript describing the events that followed a young aristocrat's attempt to assault a tavern girl, which was thwarted rather physically by her brother. More conflict follows and the brother is killed, so the girl resorts to witchcraft, raising a kind of doppelganger of her brother to protect her and avenge his death. This is one of Kirk's best short stories.

"Lex Talionis" deals with a reformed criminal who found religion but who still lives in a disreputable part of the city. It is disreputable, we are told, because urban renewal inevitably leads to decay and corruption. He is out of prison but not on parole and another thug named Butte believes that he escaped and uses that knowledge to pressure him into helping steal a large sum of money. He agrees but since our protagonist is clearly already dead, things do not go quite the way they were planned and Butte ultimately pays for his sins.

"Fate's Purse" is short and simple but well constructed. A miserly man is found dead, apparently victim of an accident. His brother inherits the property, which is supposed to have caches of money hidden about, but some time later he appears to have gone insane, insisting that his dead brother is plaguing him. He dies of shock, but only after admitting that he was present at the accident and could have saved his brother's life, but refrained from doing so in order to inherit the rumored fortune.

"An Encounter by Mortstone Pond" is a nostalgic, non-fantastic piece about a dying man's visit to his parents' graves. "Watchers at the Strait Gate" describes the visit of a habitual hobo to the elderly priest who has befriended him. The hobo has died and has returned to help the priest, who has also died, to make the transition to the afterlife.

An art thief plans to steal valuable paintings from the mansion occupied by a blind invalid in "Balgrummo's Hell." The house is falling to pieces and has been shunned for decades because of Lord Balgrummo's evil reputation from when he was younger and mobile. He underestimates his adversary, however, because the elderly man pulls him back through time to the day when he raised the devil.

In "The Princess of All Lands" a woman with psychic powers is apparently kidnapped by three people, but they are actually ghosts who do not realize that they a're dead and she separates them from Earth and sends them to Hell. "Saviourgate" is a mildly tedious piece in which a traveler discovers that he has become somewhat unglued in time for a short period.

"The Last God's Dream" is a reminiscence by a powerful politician in Yugoslavia related to a pair of American tourists in which he describes his earlier experiences and strange dreams. "There's a Long, Long Trail A-Winding" involves the hobo from "Watchers at the Strait Gate," but takes place while he is still alive. He takes shelter in a large but apparently abandoned house. He finds letters concerning the previous occupants then has what appears to be an hallucination in which he rescues them from a gang of thugs. He subsequently finds a plaque commemorating that very act, suggesting that he has visited the past, or is perhaps a ghost.

If there is an overall theme to Kirk's short fiction, it is apprehension about and resentment of most forms of change, which one might predict by reading his nonfiction. With only one or two exceptions, Kirk refrains from letting this overwhelm his narrative but he makes no effort to present a balanced view.

Kirk also wrote three novels. *Lord of the Hollow Dark* (1979) is a haunted house story that has become a collectible item commanding high prices. *Old House of Fear* (1961) is a suspense novel and *A Creature of the Twilight* (1966) is a political satire.

Old House of Fear – the best of the three - takes place on the fictional island of Carnglass off the coast of Scotland. A rich entrepreneur named MacAskival decides to buy the island because it is where his family originated and because he has ordered by his doctors to take an extended rest. He sends his lawyer, Hugh Logan, to purchase the entire island. The current owner is Ann Robertson, who calls herself Lady MacAskival, although she is not related. Although she has put off any discussion of a sale for years, she has suddenly written requesting immediate action.

Carnglass is remote, private, and its former residents – who seem to have been largely removed from the island by its current owner – were notoriously superstitious and resistant to Christianity in the early 19th Century. The main house is known as the Old House of Fear and there is a legend that someone in the environs is a legendary chess set donated by the Viking forbears of the family to propitiate some god or demon. Supposedly the house is also haunted.

Logan discovers that there is no ready means of communication with or travel to the island. While trying to make such arrangements, he is almost severely beaten by a gang of thugs and is followed by a mysterious man with a military bearing. This is Captain Gare, a cashiered soldier, who tries to bribe Logan into going home. Logan has also heard of someone named Dr. Jackman, who seems to terrify Gare.

Logan manages to get ashore in a small boat on the far side from the house, and there he sees several men pursuing another. The fugitive is named Donley, and he later shows up at the deserted cabin where Logan is sheltering, explaining that he was not willing to go along with Jackman and his gang, who have taken the elderly owner prisoner and driven off or killed all of her help. Donley takes the small boat and leaves the island, promising to call the authorities when – and if – he reaches the mainland.

Logan finds an ally when he quietly approaches the house, Mary Askival, who tells him that she was the one who wrote the note. She convinces Logan to pretend that he is her fiancé. Jackman tries to convince him to leave at the first opportunity, claiming that Mary is underage and perhaps mentally ill. Logan somewhat implausibly is swayed by Jackman's account even though he has had previous evidence aplenty that the man is up to no good. Mary tells him that Jackman is the reincarnation of the Firgower, a mythical goatlike figure who is bound to the family in legends.

A deadly cat and mouse game follows before open conflict breaks out and our heroes win the day. There is a strong atmosphere of myth and terror throughout the book, and in fact Jackman's death has some mildly ambiguous supernatural overtones, but the book is a thriller rather than horror.

A Creature of the Twilight (1966) takes Manfred Arcane as its protagonist, a character who appears in a couple of the short stories. He is a European who has become a powerful minister in the government of the fictional African nation of Hamnegri. Following the assassination of the local strong man, Arcane becomes unofficial head of state as a civil war breaks out, and the book is framed as his memoirs, describing the strange people he met during the months that followed. There is political intrigue, satire, some rather violent interludes, and commentary on the shortcomings of international diplomacy. Kirk wrote no other fiction, although he produced a substantial output of nonfiction.

Kirk's influence on the conservative political movement was considerable at the time, although present trends have moved to other concerns. He may end up being best remembered for his fiction, although it is in general competent but unremarkable.

CODY GOODFELLOW'S MYTHOS

Cody Goodfellow has written five novels and quite a few short stories, most of them horror and most from the smaller publishing houses, and his work is generally well respected. He has written the screenplay for a Lovecraft related movie as well as a number of short stories that are related to the Cthulhu Mythos, most of which have been collected as *Rapture of the Deep* (2016).

The collection opens with "The Anatomy Lesson," set in Massachusetts sometime in the 18th Century. A shortage of cadavers might delay the certification of some medical students so two of them set out to rob graves to remedy the situation. They encounter a ghoul whom they compel to lead them into its underground demesne, which includes a vast cavern and various prodigious artifacts. They are driven by the possibility of discovering some of the ghouls' secrets, including their powers of regeneration and effective immortality. One of them receives that knowledge, but in a terrible manner. This was a fair story with some effective scenes but the author may have tried too hard to emulate Lovecraft's flowery style in some passages, which contrast with the more modern prose style that predominates.

"Konig Feurio" is a much better story. A World War II German submarine is foundering in the aftermath of a mutiny when they encounter a German surface raider from the previous war, still active, but now crewed by both humans and a fishlike hybrid race, united to prey on all the nations of Earth. "To Skin a Corpse" isn't really a Mythos story despite some window dressing. The protagonists bring a dead thug back to life hoping to make him talk about where he hid some stolen money, but things rapidly get out of control. It bears some slight resemblance to "Herbert West – Reanimator," but there is no other real link to Lovecraft.

"In the Shadow of Swords" involves a United Nations inspection team in Saddam Hussein's Iraq. Shortly before they are to pack up and go home, they intercept a distress signal from a secret Iraqi installation. They also turn up a peculiar artifact which the Iraqis insist initially does not belong to them. They eventually find a storehouse filled with Sumerian antiquities and uncover a plot to open the gateways between worlds and allow the Old Ones back into our universe. This is a very good story although the use of present tense narration gives it an odd sense of artificiality.

"Garden of the Gods" is a slightly over the top Mythos story. An inhuman but intelligent creature shows up in South America and enslaves a group of people to defend it and its nest. The creature turns out to be a shuggoth. An Old One shows up and the two have a battle to the death. This is not a bad story but it has none of the feel of a traditional Mythos tale despite the obvious references. That is not necessarily a bad thing, but it may confound some readers' expectations.

"Grinding Rock" is a fairly minor piece about a firefighter who stumbles onto a sacrificial offering to keep the world safe, for a time. "Rapture of the Deep" describes the voyage of two remote viewers to the bottom of the ocean, to the lost city of R'Lyeh and the sleeping being that exists there. It is probably the most true to Lovecraft and arguably the best story in the collection.

"Inside Uncle Sid" deals with some cultists who prey on an older man who is not entirely rational. Hs niece tries rather ineffectually to help him. There are some very late references to the Mythos but they are not an important part of the story. "Archons" wanders around a bit and never really coalesces. It is the second story in the collection set in the Mideast and narrated in present tense. "Broken Sleep" deals with shared dreams and the strange creatures that can manifest themselves within them.

"Cahokia" is a radical change of pace, following the efforts of a group of people studying an anomaly in the asteroid belt where explorers have found a gateway to an alternate universe. They discover, predictably, something that they cannot handle. The final story is "Swinging," which mixes astral projection, possession, and other supernatural phenomena with Lovecraft, not very successfully.

Despite a couple of blow par stories, this was an interesting and generally rewarding collection. Goodfellow's experiments with different narrative styles and voices results in an occasionally uneven experience. He generally eschews the clichés of the Lovecraft pastiche, but he seems uncertain at times about what to put in its place.

HENRY S. WHITEHEAD

Henry S. Whitehead (1882-1932) was a Harvard graduate and Episcopal deacon when he wasn't writing short horror fiction, much of which involved elements of voodoo he picked up during a stint in the Virgin Islands. He was a friend of Howard Philips Lovecraft and a regular contributor to the pulp magazines. His stories often take a patronizing view of non-whites, whom he obviously considered culturally if not intellectually inferior, but without hostility. The narrator of many of his stories is named Gerald Canevin, although the stories themselves are unrelated otherwise. Most of his work was collected in two volumes – *West India Lights* (1946) and *Jumbee and Other Voodoo Tales* (1944), and the individual stories have since been recollected in various combinations. The most complete is *Voodoo Tales: The Ghost Stories of Henry S. Whitehead* (2012).

"Black Terror" is typical of his output. A young man of uncertain reputation has dared to fall in love with the daughter of a prosperous black merchant. The latter hires a papaloi to remove the irritant using the power of voodoo. The narrator and a white police officer lament the primitive emotions of the people involved. The author acknowledges here that voodoo's power is in the minds of its victims and is not otherwise supernatural. A Christian clergyman is able to convince the victim that God will protect him and he lives.

A painting of the execution of three pirates alters mysteriously in "West India Lights." The protagonist and a friend discover that they can ask questions and one of the painted figures will answer yes or no by closing the appropriate eye. The figure leads them to a pirate treasure and we learn that he was cursed to exist tormented in the painting until it was returned to its rightful owners. A man discovers that his friend, whom many people find inexplicably frightening, was actually sired when an orangutan raped his mother in "Williamson."

In "The Shut Room" an inn is plagued by the disappearance of shoes and other items, all of which are made of leather. One room in the inn has been kept locked for a century following a murder committed therein, and although the current landlord is not superstitious, he has kept it empty for reasons of tradition. The solution is obviously the ghost of the dead man returning and searching for a lost possession.

A fleeing murderer runs into a nest of oversized spiders in "The Left Eye," which is the name of the island where they live. "Tea Leaves" is non-fantastic. A spinster touring Europe buys a necklace for a few dollars which turns out to be worth a quarter million. A ghostly car and its occupants make an appearance in "The Napier Limousine." It transports two men magically to a rendezvous where they manage to foil a blackmail scheme.

"The Trap" involves a mysterious mirror which displays occasional odd optical effects. A student touches the glass and feels an odd sensation, and a few hours later he disappears mysteriously. The protagonist, who owns the mirror, dreams that he has had some sort of telepathic link with the missing boy. Whitehead adds some interesting variations to the world in the mirror theme, but they are not always consistent and some of the attributes of the "other dimension" are clearly designed for their ease of narration rather than to fit into any philosophical scheme.

"The Ravel Pavane" is more fantasy than horror. A musician has visions whenever she hears the music mentioned in the title. These involve a progressive move toward a room that she has never visited in reality and eventually she steps through an illusory door and enters that world. "Sea Change" is a rather unlikely story about a man subject to a degenerative disease who is marooned on an island with his wife and without his medication. He decides to swim out to sea and perish rather than let his wife see him decline, but the sea itself heals him.

"The People of Pan" is set on a supposedly deserted island which is being surveyed by a representative of a timber company. He finds the entrance to a vast underground chamber and discovers that a lost colony of Greeks is living there, worshipping Pan. His arrival triggers the end of their hidden civilization. It is a mildly dark fantasy rather than a horror story.

"The Chadbourne Episode" involves a missing child who was abducted – and eaten – by a family of ghouls. It is unusually graphic for Whitehead. "Scar-Tissue" is another fantasy, this one involving a man who remembers a previous life as a gladiator in Atlantis. "-In Case of Disaster Only" is a very minor story about a traveler at sea who hears the emergency bell ring just as his business partner on shore dies, and then discovers that the bell is inoperable.

In "Bothon" a man experiences visions of some mysterious catastrophe after suffering a minor head injury. He has odd dreams and continues to hear sounds inaudible to everyone else, sounds of terrorized people and some kind of physical conflict or disaster. A doctor friend suggests that he may be experiencing clairaudience, the psychic apprehension of sounds from another time and/or place. This turns out to be loosely connected to the Cthulhu Mythos stories of H.P. Lovecraft because the protagonist manages to identify particular words from the tumult, including a reference to R'Lyeh. He eventually realizes that he is experiencing events in the life of Bothon, who was a general serving the empire of Atlantis at the time it succumbed to an apparent cataclysm accompanied by the attack of monstrous creatures.

"The Great Circle" is one of Whitehead's longest stories. Three men land in a small plane in a circular clearing in a remote part of Mexico. A freak wind sends a jacket up into a tree and one of the men climbs up after it, but never comes down. Local Indians surround the area in large numbers but will come no closer and the two remaining men realize that they have intruded into the lair of an evil air elemental. The story becomes a really bizarre fantasy as the two explorers find themselves in another world.

"Jumbee" is Whitehead's best known story, but it is not clear why since it is far from his best. It mixes a kind of clairvoyant message from the dead with a were-canine and some other magical stuff, all in such a short narrative that it feels jumbled together rather than solidly plotted. "Cassius" is, for example, a much better story. The narrator employs a local man named Brutus on his estate in the Virgin Islands. Brutus is subject to attacks by a mysterious creature the size of a large rat that conceals itself cleverly and even makes use of simple tools to gain access to its prey. It turns out that Brutus had a parasitic twin removed from his body and this is the creature which now torments him. The creature is eventually killed by a cat.

"Black Tancrede" is a fairly creepy story about an executed pirate whose severed hand prowls a hotel generations later. "The Shadows" concerns a man who can see the shadows of things that happened in the past when the lights are dim. "Sweet Grass" is a rather routine story of a man who offends a voodoo practitioner and falls ill when she uses voodoo magic against him.

"The Tree-Man" is chronologically the earliest Canevin story, set shortly after his arrival in the Virgin Islands. He observes that some of the local people have unusually strong relationships to particular trees and observes the upset that occurs when one man's tree is to be cut down. It is more fantasy than horror. "Passing of a God" involves possession by a voodoo deity, which is normally confined to the mentally ill or physically infirm, but in this case affects a European because of a tumor he did not even suspect existed. "Hill Drums" is a non-fantastic story about a white racist who runs into difficulties in the Virgin Islands.

A woman rents a house that has long stood idle in "The Black Beast." Within a few weeks, her acquaintances begin to notice that she looks worn and worried. She confesses to the narrator that she has begun to see the shape of a bull's head on a section of blank wall, and that it has grown larger and clearer with the passage of time. The bull, which has a somewhat human face, appears to be seriously and recently injured and its image is projected out from the wall, although not visible all the time and only, so far, to the woman herself. An investigation reveals that the house was once inhabited by a family one member of whom was exposed to a voodoo ceremony in which his spirit briefly merged with that of a bull, and that the young man subsequently died horribly with his soul in a kind of magical limbo.

"Seven Turns in a Hangman's Rope" is another very long story. The protagonist finds an old painting of the hanging of a pirate named Fawcett and two of his men. The painting, although clearly the work of an amateur, is done in very great detail. After cleaning it, the painting's new owner discovers that the expression of one of the dead men has changed, a device also used in "West India Lights." The bulk of the story, however, is a flashback and a pirate story in which a free man joins the pirates after his ship is captured, leads a brief but adventurous life, and is eventually executed for his compliance – although he would certainly have died immediately if he had refused to join. There is no other fantastic content.

"Mrs. Lorriquer" is an otherwise impressive woman who rather obviously cheats at card games, even though she seems very nice and honest otherwise. It turns out that the spirit of a dead woman in the house where she lives takes possession of her when she plays cards. "The Projection of Armand Dubois" is a mildly convoluted ghost story in which a voodoo practitioner returns from the dead briefly to bother a woman he dislikes. "The Fireplace" features another ghost, this one returning to explain what really happened the night four men died in a fire. A slave bites one of the slavers in "The Lips" and a mouth, complete with teeth, develops from the wound.

His remaining stories are quite minor. "The Moon Dial" and "The Tabernacle" are both mild fantasies involving dreams. "No Eye Witnesses" involves a man's strange vision of a murder which takes place nearby, transformed into metaphorical figures. A woman returns from the dead to warn her son about poison mushrooms in "Across the Gulf" and a man has a vision of his own death in "The Door." A sailor rescues a woman from a sea creature in "Sea-Tiger."

Whitehead's dwindling reputation is not a product of his writing skills, which were generally quite good, but rather because he failed to produce any individual stories that stood out remarkably enough to draw attention to his lesser work. Readers unfamiliar with the name may well be surprised to find out just how large a volume of creditable work he did turn out during his lifetime.

THREE NOVELS OF WITCHCRAFT

Evangeline Walton and Josephine Pinckney were both accomplished novelists whose work each includes a novel of supernatural horror involving witchcraft. Josephine Pinckney (1895-1957) was a southern writer who was initially best known for her poetry, but her five novels made her one of the most popular female writers of the 1940s, though she is largely forgotten now. *Great Mischief* (1942) was a Book of the Month Club selection. Fritz Leiber (1910-1992) was a major name in science fiction and fantasy, and was also noted for his supernatural fiction, which usually broke from traditional forms. *Conjure Wife* has been filmed at least twice.

Great Mischief is set in Charleston late in the 19th Century. Timothy Partridge is a druggist who puts his faith in science. His business is marginal because his sister Penelope insists that he should not be making a great deal of money out of other people's misery. One rainy day a stranger comes into his shop, a peremptory young woman who wants a dangerous drug even though she has no prescription and who is prone to making dreamy allusions to the moon and other elements of the natural world. He finds himself providing what she asks for almost as though under compulsion.

The local doctor, Will Golightly, is Partridge's cousin. Partridge and his sister share their home with a destitute older man named Dombie. The Partridges have very different world views and sharply disagree on many issues, but they rarely talk about their differences openly. The day after his encounter with his mysterious customer, Patridge impulsively suggests that he might sell the shop and go abroad to study for a while, much to the dismay of Penelope and Dombie.

Still in an unsettled mood, Partridge finds some residue of the concoction he put together for the stranger and rubs it into his own skin. This is followed by a brief period of intense hallucinations. Long suppressed resentment begins to surface and he actually quarrels with Penelope when she asks him to help pay for an ocean voyage for a dying woman. That evening a carelessly laid fire spreads through the shop and house while he is out for a walk, and he returns to find the building in ruins, his sister and Dombie dead inside. Since he was the one who laid the fire, he was the cause of their deaths.

With the money he inherits plus the insurance, Partridge buys himself a new house in an obscure part of the city. He also tracks down his visitor and identifies her as Lucy Farr, part of a large family. He expresses his curiosity about the potion he made up for her and asks to see the formula again, but she tells him that he is "too scientific to learn anything." He makes no immediate effort to set up shop again and is troubled by lurking figures in his dreams.

He feels guilty, convinced that his carelessness caused the fire, and that it might have been intentional on some unconscious level. He stops going to church and his old acquaintances and new neighbors begin to talk about him behind his back. One night a strange woman comes to his house and accuses him directly, but she might have been just an hallucination. He finds the print of a cloven hoof in his yard and wonders if the devil has paid him a visit.

Eventually he goes secretly to consult with an elderly black woman who is supposed to have some familiarity with the occult. He purchases a charm to keep the woman from returning to his house, but she is too powerful and slips through a keyhole, materializing on the other side. She identifies herself as Sinkinda, although that is not her true name, and suggests that his sister was not the pure Christian he believed her to be and that she may have literally brought Dombie back from the dead through magical means. Partridge wonders if Lucy Farr has set Sinkinda on him, but cannot imagine how he offended her.

Partridge begins growing herbs on his property and Lucy Farr joins him, sparingly at first, but eventually they become sexually involved, although secretly. He decides that Sinkinda was a manifestation created by Lucy and confuses the two at times. He has openly abandoned his religion, convinced that he is damned anyway for having killed his sister, and Lucy encourages him toward the dark side.

One night Lucy convinces Partridge to join her for a sabbat. They use psychedelic drugs and are transported to a mansion where he is introduced to Satan. He manages to set fire to Hell itself, although Lucy tells him the next day that it was only his personal vision of Hell that he destroyed, that it is not a single place or reality.

He interprets an earthquake as the end of the world after Lucy refuses to marry him, and eventually throws himself into a chasm.

Although the supernatural events are ambiguous for most of the book, the final chapters establish that they are real. The book is less a narrative than an intellectual exchange with numerous discussions of the differences between good and evil, the relationship between God and Satan, and other associated issues. It is well crafted and poses some interesting questions, but is very limited in terms of other story values.

Evangeline Walton (1907-1996) was the pseudonym of Evangeline Wilna Ensley. She is best known for the Mabinogion tetralogy, based on Welsh mythology, which she wrote during the 1930s, although only the first saw print at the time. She revised them during the 1970s when fantasy began to emerge as a genre separate from science fiction. Her single horror novel, *Witch House*, was published by Arkham House in 1945.

Elizabeth Quincy Stone is afraid that her daughter, Betty-Ann, is connected to some possibly supernatural phenomena at their house, so she decides to employ Dr. Gaylord Carew, a famous exorcist, to clear the matter up. Stone and two cousins stand to inherit substantial fortunes from a late aunt, but only if they live in the house for ten full years beforehand. The dead woman named her home Witch House because one of her ancestors was executed for witchcraft. It stands alone on a small island. Another ancestor was a sea captain who brought home a Chinese mistress, who reputedly conducted strange rituals in the house.

The cousins are Joseph Lee – who now calls himself Joseph Quincy - and Quincy Lee, brothers of the Chinese woman's half-American son. Joseph is unmarried but Quincy has a wife named Zoia. Stone went against her aunt's wishes and married a man who subsequently killed himself when he lost all of his money and felt he could not support his wife and child. Betty-Ann has not been told that her father committed suicide, but she has begun seeing frightening figures in the house, including a huge hare. Hares are, according to local legend, frequently connected to witches. Two of the girl's pets, a dog and a cat, were both found dead and mutilated under mysterious circumstances.

There are brief side trips to develop the history of the family, and also to explain Carew's knowledge of the occult. He agrees to spend at least several days at Witch House to address the problem, but first makes some tentative attempts to learn more about its current residents. Quincy Lee appears to have occult interests of his own, although it sounds as though he is more a dilettante than a skilled practitioner. Carew also learns that Elizabeth Stone was thought by some to have used witchcraft to entice her husband to elope with her. Zoia Lee is descended from one of Rasputin's followers and is reportedly very susceptible to hypnotism.

It is Zoia who meets him when he first arrives, and she takes great pains to present her version of an incident in which Betty-Ann supposedly attacked a painting of the dead aunt with a knife and was restrained by Quincy. Elizabeth apparently believed that he had attacked her daughter for some reason. Carew senses a malevolent presence almost from the moment he enters the house, but cannot immediately identify its source or nature.

The very first evening he observes what is clearly poltergeist phenomena and actually sees the phantom hare as well. His acceptance of these things causes an immediate connection with Betty-Ann. His early supposition is that the house does retain images and emotions which the girl is able to perceive, in fact is unable to avoid perceiving. He also believes that she has an unconscious telekinetic power and is probably responsible – though without knowing it – for the physical damage and disappearing objects. He does not, however, believe in ghosts and he offers no explanation for the vision of the black hare. While he is skeptical of the possibility of the dead lingering in the world of the living, he accepts the possibility that the aunt may have used "black magic" to ensure that her enmity permeated the house.

After several days, the incidents become less frequent, but Carew knows that it is the lull before the storm. One night he wakens, convinced that his mission is hopeless and that he should leave the house immediately, but he recognizes that the thoughts are not his own, are being placed into his mind by an external force. Then Betty-Ann has a vivid and frightening dream in which she is abducted by the hare, but Carew uses reassurance and hypnotism to calm her down.

A time of relative peace follows, although for some reason Quincy seems angry and preoccupied. Carew believes that the evil force will not be content to simply drive him away now but must score some tangible victory to destroy Betty-Ann's faith in his power to protect her. Carew also feels himself being drawn toward Elizabeth but it is not clear whether or not his emotions are his own or are being imposed upon him.

A crisis seems imminent and Quincy Lee is killed in an inexplicable rockslide right in front of the others. His wife claims that she was supposed to lure Carew to that spot, unaware that she was supposed to die with him. She is injured and dies a short time later. Carew proves to Betty-Ann that the visions she sees are contrived by another mind to frighten her, but he fails to anticipate that their creator – Joseph – will move instead against the girl's mother. Carew realizes the truth in time, rescues Elizabeth, and sets the house on fire. Joseph dies in the conflagration.

This is more than a simple story of witchcraft and a haunted house. The various characters engage in thought provoking debates about the nature of reality, of personal obligations, of destiny, and other issues. The characters are also unusually deeply drawn. This is a minor classic which has been reprinted a half dozen times since its first appearance.

The best known of the three novels is *Conjure Wife* (1952) by Fritz Leiber, which was filmed as *Burn Witch Burn* (1962) and later as *Witches' Brew* (1980), although the latter was uncredited . Norman Saylor is a professor of ethnology at Hempnell College. His wife Tansy is, as far as he is concerned, a very conventional and not particularly imaginative woman. He considers her a lucky charm, however, because she has quietly helped him through a number of minor career problems and has settled in as a very effective faculty wife. Their life seems almost perfect until the day he pokes around in her dressing room and finds artifacts suggesting that she believes in and practices witchcraft.

Since Norman is a conceited chauvinist, he insists that Tansy destroy all of her protective charms and stop playing with magic. She admits that she has never been completely sure that any of it was real, but she also is convinced that some of the other faculty wives are using magic as well, and that several of them hate her husband. Within minutes of the destruction of the last of the charms, Norman receives a threatening call from a disgruntled student and a seductive one from an unknown and clearly disturbed woman. It never occurs to him that there might be a connection to his precipitous action.

The following day is even worse. A female student accuses him of having seduced her. He is questioned about a party he attended which was hosted by people with a suspect background. He is more frank in class than usual and offends the daughter of the college president and he absentmindedly breaks a rule about faculty smoking on the grounds. And there is a rumor that one of his own published papers was plagiarized. His round of "bad luck" continues. He catches a brief glimpse of what appears to be a shadowy outline of an animal, and he notices habits of three of the faculty wives which remind him somehow of primitive magical rituals. He even briefly wonders if witchcraft is possible after all.

Having given up her own magic, Tansy is now susceptible to the evil spells of her rivals and Norman ultimately has to recognize that he was wrong. In fact, he consults another witch in order to find out how to cast his own spells in order to safeguard her and restore something of the life they had been living before his discovery.

The story is told from Norman's viewpoint, which might have been a mild error because he is so obtuse and opinionated for most of the story that the reader may be pardoned for thinking he is only getting what he deserves. Otherwise, this is still the novel of contemporary witchcraft against which all others must be judged, and most will be found wanting.

SARBAN

Sarban was the pseudonym used by John William Wall (1910-1989), a British diplomat whose writing career was very short, consisting of three novels and a handful of short stories, all published in the early 1950s. Several of his stories are only available in high priced collectors' editions, now out of print, and almost impossible to find.

His first book was *Ringstones and Other Curious Tales* (1951), which contains the title novel and four short stories. The stories were left out of the paperback versions published during the 1960s. The first of these was "A Christmas Story." During a Christmas party a Russian expatriate tells a story about an adventure he had as a young man. He and another soldier were stranded in a remote part of near Arctic Russia when they were rescued by primitive tribesmen native to the area. The meat which is given to them has a strange taste and they eventually discover that the tribe hunts the last few mammoths that still live in that remote region.

"Capra" is also in the form of a reminiscence. The narrator recalls an old acquaintance who was seriously wounded in the war and remained in poor health afterward. He had married an attractive younger woman, but they were seen in the company of a dashing and mildly offensive man her own age named Falzon who is from Argentina but was staying in Greece at the time. They are off to visit a rich Greek whose mansion is near an area reputed to be home to wild goats, which the soldier, Tommy Lobeck, hopes to hunt.

Falzon plays a cruel and elaborate hoax on Lobeck, then arranges a costume party at which he appears as Pan. The narrator suspects that murder is in the air and follows the wife when she goes out to the garden, there to encounter a satyr-like figure whom he presumes to be Falzon. Lobeck appears with a gun and shoots the satyr who, wounded, runs off. To the narrator's surprise, Falzon is still in the house, uninjured, and the trail of blood leads to a cliff overlooking the ocean. This is a superbly written story, one of the best depictions of the cuckolded husband cracking under the pressure.

"Calmahain" opens with two rather neglected children playing an elaborate fantasy game on the extensive grounds of the house where they are living. Each creates an imaginary adventure and relates it to the other. One of these involves an encounter with a barbaric people who are holding some young slaves from a distant land called Calmahain. They decide to merge their two stories and take an imaginary journey by boat to rescue the slaves and return them to their homeland. The adults with whom they are living forbid them to continue their game but an air raid destroys the house and the children are never found, although it is implied that they set sail on the model boat they built and have disappeared into their fantasy.

"The Khan" is another story told by one of the characters. A Norwegian man is employed supervising a construction crew in Iran. His bored wife takes a young bear as a pet, much to his consternation. A short time later she is stranded in the wilderness and discovers a woman living in a strange arrangement with an adult bear. It is the weakest of the stories but, like the others, excels at presenting a physical description of the setting and characters.

Ringstones is quite short for a novel. Daphne Hazel is a university student who applies for and is hired into a temporary position looking after three children in a remote part of England. The man who employs her, Dr. Ravelin, explains that they are just learning English and that she is to help them learn the language rather than provide formal education. She arrives at the Ringstones estate and is greeted rather dourly by Mrs. Sarkissian, the housekeeper. She introduces Hazel to the boy, Nuaman, and the girls, Marvan and Ianthe. Mr. Sarkissian is the butler.

At first everything seems perfect, although no one talks much about the children and Hazel cannot discover where they are from. Dr. Ravelin provides a history of the house, which was built on a spot that has been in use in one fashion or another for centuries and which has some faint links to supposed magical activities in the distant past.

Nuaman is surprisingly adept at physical and mental challenges and the two sisters seem to have subordinated themselves to him. Katia, the maid, is similarly entranced although her broken English – she is a displaced person from Poland thanks to the war – makes it difficult for Hazel to understand the relationship. On one occasion they have a picnic at a set of standing stones nearby where Dr. Ravelin, who quietly defers to Nuaman, theorizes that the stones were erected on a place already sacred, perhaps the habitat of fairies. Katia refers to Nuaman as "No Man", which is also suggestive, and hints that his power over her and the sisters may have its sinister side.

One day she decides to cross the moor to the nearest town, despite Nuaman's entreaties for her not to go. Apparently resigned to the inevitable, he gives her directions, but she becomes lost – possibly because he misled her – and one portion of the moor strikes her as almost consciously evil. She discovers at last that she has walked in a great circle and is back where she started.

Dr. Ravelin talks about fairies and suggests they might have been an older race supplanted by humanity but never completely destroyed. They are little more than memories now but "once they were powerful and feared." Hazel is also puzzled by contradictions in what the sisters were wearing and where they were amusing themselves while she was gone, but she is too tired to pursue the matter.

That night she dreams that she is awakened by hammering. She investigates and finds Nuaman and several strange boys similar to himself building a chariot in one of the out buildings. Or is it a dream? She is never quite certain whether or not it was a real event, although she tells herself that it could not have actually happened. She also examines a map of the moor and cannot figure out how she could possibly have strayed from the marked path. Katia tells her that "the road hide itself."

Katia also reveals that she is afraid of Nuaman, that she believes that he will keep her and Hazel at Ringstones for a hundred years. She also fleetingly mentions the demons of the forest. Dr. Ravelin tells Hazel that Katia still believes in the legend of the Elf-King and the differential time scales between our world and the world of faerie.

Dr. Ravelin leaves to conduct some business and Hazel feels her first flutter of worry that she is in over her head, that Ringstones holds a secret that has more than an element of menace. That night she awakens in a near panic and quietly dresses, packs a few things, and sets out to leave Ringstones behind. She plans to follow the road this time, even though it is longer, but when she leaves the estate she discovers that the road has been diverted. It now leads to the standing stones and there is no trace of a route to anywhere else.

There are literally dozens of young men and women around, none of whom she has ever seen before. Mr. Sarkissian cuffs her and leads her back, reprimanding her for causing him trouble. She and Katia are to be placed in harness to the newly built chariot but the diary ends at that point.

We return to the frame story in which two men are discussing the diary. Nu'man is a legendary figure identified with the Greek god Adonis, whose role in Greece was varied but generally associated with vegetation and youth. The two men are convinced that Hazel was writing a work of fiction, but doubts linger so they decide to visit Ringstones and ask Hazel about what she wrote. They find Ringstones in ruins, apparently a decay of long standing, and Hazel working in a nearby town. Her situation is very similar to that in the book, teaching foreign children to speak English, and she claims that she invented the entire story but that a cover letter explaining the nature of her manuscript was not mailed in a timely manner.

She also explains that she and her employer had been for a walk on the moor one day when she sprained her ankle. He had helped her as far as Ringstones where she could take shelter while he went for help. The story she wrote was the result of dreams she had while waiting for rescue, incorporating other events that had happened earlier. But there is evidence that her dream was in some way real and that if her employer had not returned in time, she would have been whisked away to the land of the Elf-King.

The novel is only marginally horror, more properly a dark fantasy. It has very little melodrama and relies upon the slow development of an atmosphere of strangeness rather than terror, although the ultimate consequences which Hazel escapes are indeed terrifying. The parallels between what really happened and how she interpreted them in her dream story are well constructed and while there is some ambiguity at the conclusion, it is clear that something supernatural was indeed involved.

Sarban's second novel was *The Sound of His Horn* (1952), which is better known in part because it is an alternate history science fiction story as well as horror. The premise of this short novel is that the Nazis won World War II and essentially rule the world, although we are only shown this through a very narrow and odd perspective.

The narrator is a friend of Alan Querdillon, the protagonist, who was released from a prisoner of war camp after the German surrender in 1945. His family and friends notice a decided difference in his personality, as though he was eternally preoccupied, part of his mind still back in his cell. During an argument about the morality of fox hunting, he unexpectedly remarks that "terror" is the most memorable part of a hunt.

Once again Sarban casts the story as one being recounted between two characters. Querdillon tells the narrator of his escape from the camp and his arduous journey cross country. He stumbles upon some sort of fence or barrier and is shocked into unconsciousness. When he wakens, his hands are bandaged and he is in bed, tended to by nurses who will not tell him where he is or how he got there.

Eventually he discovers that he is in an alternate future in which Germany dominates the world and breeds the "lesser" races for sport or servants or both. Querdillon has not yet met his host, Count van Halkenberg, who seems to spend most of his time hunting, but he does notice that his entire staff seems terrified, even the doctor who is treating him. He also begins to wonder about the animals the Count uses in hunting, which sound particularly fierce, although he has never seen any of them.

The German hierarchy now breeds humans as hunting animals, and as animals to be hunted, in the latter case mostly nubile young women. Querdillon reacts in horror and his distaste is obvious, but eventually he becomes the object of a hunt himself. During the course of this hunt, he somehow is transported back to the present world. He ascribes this to madness rather than actual travel to another reality, but it is clear that he believes that he really visited a Nazi land of horror. This is probably the most brutal portrayal of a Nazi victory in all of the many books written on the subject.

The Doll Maker (1953) was the author's last book. Clare Lydgate is eighteen years old but since her father is working out a contract in Malaya, she has been staying at a remote private school, Paston Hall, where she is preparing for Oxford University. Despite the school's assurances that the students are free to visit the nearby woods and town, in fact that is not the case and she chafes at the restrictions, particularly after the tutor hired to help her prepare dies unexpectedly. She becomes almost immediately a confirmed rebel.

Paston Hall is rented from the Sterne family, who live in seclusion on the other side of a very tall brick wall. One night Clare sneaks out and climbs the wall, then accidentally dislodges a stone and finds herself dangling over the wrong side of the wall. An unknown young man helps her down and then back over the wall. The incident seems unimportant but a short time later Mrs. Sterne invites the school to send any remaining staff and senior students to take tea with her on Christmas Eve. Clare is the only senior and Mrs. Geary, a quiet and rather mousy teacher, is the only member of the staff with no previous commitments.

Mrs. Sterne is a widow living with her son Niall, who is the man Clare encountered during her misadventure. Niall is fond of muttering incantations at times and Clare believes that he is pretending to believe in magic. She also learns that the Sternes had employed a maid named Janet but that she died, apparently of the same disease as her late tutor. And both were about the same age. Niall tells her a bit about his family's history, which includes a retired traveler who experimented with growing miniature trees before his death. Niall himself admits to crafting puppets or dolls to amuse himself.

Mrs. Sterne offers to tutor Clare with Latin and this leads to regular visits, during one of which Niall shows her a miniature park with dwarf trees. He tells her that he harvests a few of the trees, which have magical properties, in order to construct his puppets. After a few weeks, Niall goes away on an unspecified business trip and Clare begins to have disturbing dreams. While he is gone, his mother burns the Christmas tree decorations including one of his dolls, which had been fastened to the tree. Clare rescues it and learns that it was a family custom, possibly a holdover from when Druids sacrificed people to their gods. She is allowed to take the doll away with her.

Niall has always insisted they were puppets and when he returns, Clare asks to see them animated. He agrees to show her, but only if she sneaks over the wall at night a week later. She realizes that she has fallen in love with him, but still jokes about his "necromantic" powers. The doll puzzles her, however, because it seems like a statue with immovable limbs and she cannot imagine how it could possibly have been intended to be animated.

The "puppet" show that Niall performs for Clare is elaborate, involving many lifelike but very small figures who walk through the miniature forest she had viewed earlier. That same night she playfully allows him to conduct a spell that will bind her to him, although she doesn't take it seriously. But she is vaguely troubled when she sees the newspaper obituary of a young woman who died of polio (called infantile paralysis at the time) just as did her tutor and the Sternes' maid. The face looks familiar, and she eventually realizes she saw it mirrored in the Christmas doll. But when she takes out the doll itself, she discovers that the wood has mysteriously fractured and decayed. He explains that he sometimes uses photographs in the newspapers instead of living models.

Clare learns that another girl was sighted out at night, returning from the direction of the Sternes' house. She believes it was Jennifer Gray, who has a rebellious streak, and is concerned that she will get caught and that this will lead to the closing off of her secret escape route – an unsecured window. When she confronts her, however, she had a shock. Gray knows about the miniature figures and implies that they are not dolls after all and that Niall is a sorcerer.

Clare realizes that she and Jennifer have both been played for fools, and that Niall is positively dangerous. She confronts him, initially convinced that he is just playing with the emotions of the women he encounters, but he confesses that he has the power to transfer their spirits into the dolls that he creates. She and Jennifer both fall ill shortly thereafter, but Clare recovers enough to sneak out of Paston Hall, climb the wall, enter Niall's workshop, and destroy the two dolls he has been working on. Niall returns and she leaves in a panic, overturning a lamp which sets the house on fire, destroying the dolls and killing him.

This was Sarban's longest and most accomplished piece of fiction, with a good deal of quietly developed suspense, strong characters, his usual gift for evoking the physical setting, and superior dialogue. It is a shame that he gave up his writing while he was still demonstrating obvious signs of improvement over his craft.

THE JOHN SILENCE STORIES

Algernon Blackwood (1869-1951) was a prolific British writer of fiction, most of it horror or dark fantasy. The first five John Silence stories were published as *John Silence, Physician Extraordinary* (1908) and an additional tale appeared in *Day and Night Stories* (1917). Silence is an occult detective who uses psychic powers to solve mysteries involving the supernatural. The terms involving the paranormal were somewhat fluid at the time Blackwood was writing, so while he is described as a clairvoyant, there is an element of telepathy as well.

The first story was "A Psychical Invasion." Silence is a physician who only takes cases that interest him and that have an unusual character. He believes that clairvoyance is "nothing more than a keen power of visualizing," but insists that the true clairvoyant "deplores his power, realizing that it adds a new horror to life." He eschews what he considers unnecessary aids like tea reading or crystal ball gazing, believing instead that thought can act at a distance and affect material objects.

In his first case he is called to investigate the circumstances in which Felix Pender has lost his sense of humor. This is serious because Pender makes his living by writing humorous stories. Pender's wife explains that he has recently begun to suggest that there is an unseen presence in the house and that it has warped his sense of humor so that he finds himself writing stories about debased characters who live tragic or squalid lives.

Silence immediately perceives that Pender's aura has been affected by a drug. Pender agrees, indicating that he took a drug experimentally on one occasion, hoping to stimulate his sense of humor, but that instead he began to sense the presence of an evil but unseen and immaterial woman. Silence explains that sometimes the unconscious residue of powerful personalities can be bound to a physical location and even act as though it was a conscious being.

After convincing the Penders to temporarily lodge elsewhere, Silence moves into their house with a cat and a dog, both of which seem sensitive to the alien influence. The dog is disturbed by an unseen presence, but the cat actually seems to welcome it. Silence, who cannot understand why his own psychic sensitivity is not working, remains unable to perceive the intruder. After awhile, the animals seem to be reacting to multiple presences and while Silence cannot determine their nature, he begins to feel pressure exerted against his own state of mind.

Silence experiences a series of hallucinations, but his will is strong enough to hold fast and eventually he is left in peace. He believes that he may have siphoned off the evil force, but he cannot be certain and recommends that the house be torn down. It was erected on the site of an earlier home where a particularly evil woman lived in the 18th Century. She was hanged for her crimes, which probably included witchcraft. The story is unusual in that most of it consists of descriptions of the reactions of the cat and the dog rather than the human characters.

The second John Silence story was "Ancient Sorceries." It is one of the undeniable classics of the horror genre. A rather diffident Englishman impulsively gets off a train in a small French village despite a veiled warning from one of the other passengers. He finds the local people a bit odd at first, and they often remind him of cats by the way they move or their expressions. He is puzzled by the atmosphere in the town and stays on for several days, during which period he realizes that he is constantly watched, that the townspeople only pretend to be normal. He suspects they act differently at night, but his inn locks its doors early and he finds himself falling into a deep sleep despite efforts to remain awake. Despite its strangeness, the town has a strange power and when he realizes it is time to leave, he finds that he cannot summon the will to do so.

His fascination with the town increases when his landlady's daughter Ilse returns from some unexplained trip. He is immediately captivated by her, although he senses once again that she is concealing a dark secret. On one occasion she happens upon a pile of burning leaves and runs away in obvious panic, although she makes little of it later. He eventually declares himself in love with Ilse, who tells him that this is a step necessary for him to embrace the real life of the town, which is still in touch with ancient powers. She also insists that she drew him to come there by some mysterious telepathic power and that she is the commander of his soul.

He decides once again to leave but still cannot summon the strength to do so. But that night he finally observes the townspeople in the darkness. They all emerge from their houses, get down on hands and knees, and are transformed into oversized cats. He follows them and discovers that they are engaged in a magical ritual that allows them to commune with the spirits that ruled the world long ago. Eventually he realizes his peril and lights a fire to ward off the transformed townspeople while he makes his escape.

John Silence is almost an afterthought in this tale, although it is he to whom the story is being related. At the end, he discusses the matter with a third party and reveals that the bewitched man's ancestors had once lived in that very same town, which was notorious for its toleration of witchcraft. But he believes that the story was actually a delusion, that his client was possibly reliving experiences from an earlier life, but that in the present the town was perfectly ordinary. There remains, however, a note of ambiguity. There have been other stories of mysterious towns with dark secrets – Robert Aickman, Stephen King, and many others have found the premise useful. Blackwood, however, has written the archetypal story in this area.

The narrator, Hubbard, accompanies Silence on his next case, "The Nemesis of Fire." Retired Colonel Wragge has written about an unspecified problem in the house where he lives with his invalid sister. Both visitors sense a kind of mental heat that neither has previously experienced. The previous owner, his brother, died mysteriously with his face disfigured as though scorched by a very hot fire. His death and that of another man are linked to a small section of forest near the house.

There has been a rash of strange phenomena recently. Invisible creatures are heard moving in the woods or have been chased by dogs. A series of small grass fires has occurred with no apparent origin. None of the local people will venture into the woods, even during the daylight. Recently fires have started inside the house, always in the sister's room but always when she is elsewhere. Wragge has avoided telling her about the other incidents.

Hubbard and Silence are exploring the woods when they see a point of fire moving across a pond, raising a cloud of steam. They realize it is headed toward Wragge's house and follow in time to help extinguish a fire in one of the outbuildings. During the excitement the sister, who has been confined to a wheelchair for many years, leaps up and runs across the lawn. Silence announces that the cause of the disturbance is a fire elemental. He explains that it is a conscious but immaterial force that draws its power from the properties of fire, but he does not know why this one has become so enraged that it openly attacks people and property. He is sure that there is some other intelligence directing it.

Silence proposes that a bowl of pig's blood be provided, since this is a means by which an elemental may be temporarily bound in material form. The procedure works and Wragge is temporarily possessed by the guiding spirit, who makes several references to ancient Egypt before vanishing. Silence explains that Wragge's brother had brought a mummy from Egypt before realizing that its spirit was still active. He buried it somewhere in the wooded area, which is where the grass fires occurred.

They locate the chamber where the mummy was reinterred and Silence realizes that a piece of magical jewelry was stolen from the corpse by Wragge's sister. She reappears and he orders her to replace it, but in the process of doing so she is killed, burnt to death by the elemental. This is the most suspenseful of the first three stories and some of the latter scenes are genuinely creepy.

"Secret Worship" is comparatively minor. An Englishman traveling in Europe decides to visit the strict religious school in Germany which he attended as a boy. He is told that the building has been abandoned but he ignores the warnings. When he arrives, the school is much as he remembered it, except that there are no students about. The men who ran it are still there and invite him inside, and he is struck by how closely they resemble the staff decades earlier. When they begin talking about his voluntary sacrifice, he begins to sense that he is in danger and only escapes because he invokes God's name at a critical moment, and because John Silence knew that he was coming there and used his powers to break the man's trance. The building was burnt to the ground long ago despite what he thinks he saw, after the people running it were exposed as devil worshippers.

"The Camp of the Dog" is again narrated by Hubbard, who is part of a vacation party in the islands near Sweden. John Silence is to join them after finishing up a case on the continent. Among the party is Timothy Maloney, a minister, along with his wife and his adult daughter Joan. Another is Pete Sangree, an amiable young man. Joan is the most at ease in the wilderness and Sangree has a quiet but obvious fixation on her. Joan, however, confides to Hubbard that she feels that there is something dreadful buried in his personality, a flaw of which even he is unaware.

The first hint of something wrong is when Joan's sleep is disturbed one night by the sound of some large animal prowling around the camp. There are tracks between her tent and Sangree's, but nowhere else. Hubbard reflects upon the fact that they are on a tiny deserted island that has no wildlife and cannot imagine where the animal might have come from. Two nights later it tears a hole in Joan's tent before being chased away by her screams.

Hubbard spots the creature – which resembles a wolf – and follows it into Sangree's tent. Sangree is asleep, but the creature has vanished, obviously reincorporating itself into his body, although Hubbard unaccountably does not realize this. He does suspect the supernatural, however, so John Silence's arrival is a welcome event. He is immediately advised of the sequence of events.

Silence tells Hubbard that it is possible for someone to develop a second body, astrally projected, which reflects his or her inner nature. He characterizes recent events as lycanthropy, although it is hardly a traditional werewolf that menaces the party. In fact, Silence concludes that Joan and Sangree are in love through their astral selves and he helps manipulate things so that they can be united peacefully on that level, so that their duplicate selves can merge back into their material bodies.

This is probably the weakest of the six stories. It takes quite a long time for the plot to start moving and the resolution is not entirely rationalized. The twist on the werewolf theme is interesting, however, and the story remains worthwhile.

The final John Silence story, published after the original volume, was "A Victim of Higher Space." John Silence's butler tells him that he has a peculiar visitor, so thin he can hardly be seen, so silent that he cannot be heard without the expenditure of much effort. The visitor, Racine Mudge, explains that he has spent much of his life studying higher space, which the reader might think of in contemporary terms as another dimension. He asserts, for example, that there is always a hidden way into an entirely closed space. One could enter a bubble without piercing its skin.

His studies led to the contemplation of how another dimension might appear to human senses. One day, without realizing it, Mudge crossed into an extra dimensional world. Although he was able to return to our reality, he found himself drifting back and forth on several further occasions. Silence tells him that he must mentally block the entrances between worlds but before that process can be completed, Mudge disappears right before his eyes. Fortunately, he later sends a message from the other side of the world indicating that he has returned and successfully blocked the passageways behind him.

This is a minor story but quite well done. It is a shame that Blackwood did not chronicle further adventures of John Silence, considering how prolific he was. Much of his other work bears considerable similarity in theme and structure, however, and one can almost imagine Silence appearing in many of them.

D.K. BROSTER

Dorothy Kathleen Broster (1877-1950) was known mostly during her lifetime for her historical novels, but she took time from that endeavor to write a handful of horror stories as well. She served as a British army nurse during World War II and wrote her first two books in collaboration with a co-worker before returning to civilian life. Her most famous story is "Couching at the Door."

The supernatural element in "Couching at the Door" is never explained. Augustine Marchant is a rather conceited poet living in the late 19th Century who notices one day what he believes to be a bit of fluff on the floor of his library. He makes a mental note to mention it to his housekeeper because he has very high standards about cleanliness and order. Marchant's poetry was widely regarded as salacious, but his inheritance of a substantial estate and his willingness to spend money have overcome the resistance his neighbors might otherwise have felt to being found in his company.

A short time later he notices the fluff crawling up the blanket covering his lap and decides it must be some kind of insect. He shakes it off and relocates, telling the staff to sweep the library. But as he sits outside, he sees the indistinct spot of matter moving toward him and he overcomes his disgust long enough to pick it up and throw it into a fountain, presumably to drown.

Marchant travels to London where that evening he sees a three foot long furry caterpillar emerge from under his bed. He attempts to kill it with a fire iron but with no effect until he finally gathers it up and throws it into the fire where it vanishes, leaving behind only a faint hint of burnt hair, although it reappears a short time later, apparently unaffected. He is severely shaken by the experience and decides to visit a friend in the country before returning home. Marchant alternately thinks it was real and that it was a product of her overactive imagination.

He initially relaxes when he reaches his friend's house, but then he begins to catch glimpses of the thing once again, and at one point it brushes against him with something mimicking affection. He returns to his home and finds it waiting for him, almost welcoming him in fact, and he realizes that there is no point in attempting to destroy it because it will just reconstitute itself. Although he is an atheist, he refers to the Bible and finds a passage that warns that if a person sins, then sin itself "coucheth at the door" and that he must rule over that sin, although he doesn't entirely understand what this means.

Marchant invites a young artist, Lawrence Storey, to come for a protracted visit. Assuming that he is the master of the creature, Marchant orders it to go to Storey, but the attempt fails, at least partially. Storey seems sympathetic to Marchant's excesses and he begins to catch glimpses of what he believes to be a cat. Marchant – who has begun to think the manifestation is linked to his murder of a prostitute years earlier - arranges for him to travel to Europe and kill a prostitute of his own, and the day that it is to have occurred, he wakes up to discover that he is apparently no longer haunted.

He receives letters from Storey, whose torment has taken a very different form. No matter where he is, he sees the furniture from the room where he committed his crime, and has recurring difficulty in finding his way about amid the visual confusion. Storey drowns, either a suicide or led into the river by his hallucinations, but Marchant feels safe until a few hours later when his own creature returns, still wet from the river but larger and more malevolent than ever.

There is no precise explanation of the creature that troubles Marchant, but it is clearly linked to his mistreatment of a woman who owned a fur boa that somewhat resembles his tormentor, and at one point he confides to Storey that he may have caused her death. There is also a passing reference to his having dabbled in black magic, although he did not believe it to be real. The story is an enduring classic that evokes quite strong sensations of horror and retribution without the overt excesses of modern supernatural fiction.

"From the Abyss" uses an unnecessary but common frame to tell the story of Daphne Lawrence. The narrator of the specific tale tells the narrator of the frame story that he was once engaged to Daphne. She had gone to Europe on a vacation and was thrown from a car that went off a cliff in a deep canyon, killing the driver. The terrain is so severe that the body was not recovered. Daphne had only minor injuries but was shocked by the man's death and announced that she was returning to England.

Daphne was knocked unconscious during the accident and has a recurring sensation that she also went over the cliff in the doomed car. She has recurring dreams of climbing back up to the roadway and she informs her fiancé that the wedding is off. The situation remains unchanged until a letter arrives from France reporting that a young woman with amnesia has been found who claims to have been in the car when it went over the cliff. She also insists that she climbed back to safety.

The narrator goes to France to talk to her, but she has disappeared. While there he learns that Daphne has also left England, en route to the same part of France. He finds both versions of Daphne together at the spot where the accident occurred, and she – or they – jump to their death in front of him. This is one of the best doppelgangers stories ever written and it is surprising that it is not better known.

"Clairvoyance" is a haunted house story that is structurally unusual. It opens with a couple considering the purchase of an empty house until the wife experiences strange emotions when she sees a stain on a rug in the library. We then slip back in time to find out what happened five years previously. An experiment in hypnotism causes a teenaged girl to be possessed by the personality of a Japanese warriors and she/he kills two people before the possession ends with her own death. Although well written, the story is not up to the standard of the first two.

"The Window" takes a while to get started. The protagonist becomes infatuated with a young woman whom he has recently met, but circumstances send them their separate ways. The first World War breaks out and he is sent to France, but while there he travels to the estate which she and her brother own – which is currently untenanted – ostensibly to paint some landscapes, although he hopes vainly to encounter her there.

He starts to paint inside the abandoned house, but has the uncanny feeling that he is not alone. The atmosphere seems close so he decides to open one of the massive windows, but it unexpectedly comes loose and falls, pinning his arms under its weight and knocking him unconscious for a time. He is unable to free himself and resigns himself to a painful death, but he is saved when the brother and sister happen to come by the house in the nick of time. It turns out that one of his ancestors decapitated one of theirs and threw the head through that very window, so the window was exacting revenge. The supernatural content is minor, but the story is quite good.

"Juggernaut" concerns a haunted bath chair, which is a kind of rickshaw used to ferry tourists back and forth on a British beach. Flora Halkett is a novelist recovering from a badly sprained ankle, accompanied by her niece Primrose. They notice that one of the bath chairs is pulled by an elderly man who always looks as though he is straining even though the seat is empty. One day they ask for his services but he insists that Mrs. Birling wouldn't like it.

Curious, they ask around and discover that the man's name is Cotton and that the late Mrs. Birling, a rather obnoxious woman, employed him regularly when she was alive and left him a substantial legacy. But Cotton has been rather strange ever since, constantly pulling the chair but never taking on a customer. He is convinced she is still present because she died in his chair, suffering a heart attack, and while he had her medicine in his possession, he withheld it because he knew he was mentioned in her will. Having confessed this, he throws himself into the sea. This is psychological rather than supernatural horror, since there is no evidence that there is actually a ghost, but the outcome is the same.

"The Promised Land" is also psychological horror. Ellen Wright is finally taking her planned tour of Europe and she is discovering that it is not living up to her expectations, in part because her companions are less than agreeable people. Although she has known her for years, she realizes that she has come to hate her companion passionately. Eventually murder results, but Ellen is so out of touch with reality that she misinterprets what she has done and the way in which people react to it.

At the opening of "The Pestering" Evadne Seton and her husband purchase a small house in the country after the war because the air of London is bad for his damaged lungs. The house has changed hands with considerable frequency in recent years, but seems to be sound and comfortable. To supplement their meager income, they put up a sign and serve tea and baked goods to people who pass by on their way to the more touristy areas.

One evening Evadne is alone when someone knocks on the door. It is a lone man who insists he is there to pick up a chest rather than a prospective customer. Evadne, naturally, has no idea what he could be talking about. The hired girl is next to see the man, and she promptly quits her job and has to be driven home in tears. She bemoans the fact that the visitations have started up again but refuses to explain.

Several incidents follow and the Setons realize that they are dealing with a ghost who wants to search their house for a chest, which they are quite certain is not on the premises. The manifestations grow increasingly frightening with the passage of time and they begin to investigate possible magical remedies or exorcisms. Seton brings in a construction manager who finds a secret room. There is no chest in it, but a box containing the statue of a woman with a knife in its chest. The ghostly visitor removes the knife and that brings the haunting to an end after one final manifestation.

"The Taste of Pomegranates" is based on the legend of Persephone. Two English women are touring France and stop to examine some cave paintings, but part of the cave collapses and they are trapped. They are surprised that there are no sounds of a rescue party even hours later, and in due course they begin to suspect that they have somehow retrogressed through time, particularly when they spot a cave bear that is extinct in their own time. One of them eventually finds her way out, and the rescue party in the present finds their camera, which has been chewed by an animal with enormous teeth.

Horror was not Broster's main interest in literature. She was much more comfortable, and successful, with her historical novels. It is our loss, however, because the quality of these stories is exceptionally high and she could easily have become one of the major writers in the genre if she had persisted.

AMELIA B. EDWARDS

Amelia Ann Blandford Edwards (1831-1892) was a noted British novelist and Egyptologist. She wrote a considerable body of short supernatural fiction, although no novels, of which the most famous is "The Phantom Coach." Some of her stories were wrongly attributed to Charles Dickens until comparatively recently.

"Monsieur Maurice" is a novelette, presented as the recollections of a woman who as a child in 1819 Germany lived with her father, who was a semi-retired military officer. The father has been assigned responsibility for a prisoner of state, i.e., one who must be confined but who should be treated well. The prisoner is known to them only as Mr. Maurice, an ex-soldier and a Frenchman, who has given his parole and thus is allowed freedom to move about the compound.

Young Gretchen and Maurice become good friends and he tells her bits and pieces of his past adventures. One day he attempts to escape after withdrawing his parole, and a mysterious figure appears to interfere with a guard who attempts to shoot him. Some weeks later, an attendant poisons a glass of water, but the mystery man appears again – this time materializing out of nowhere – and knocks the glass to the floor. The poisoner and the narrator see him clearly but Maurice does not. Only at the end do we realize that this was the ghost of a man who once was employed as Maurice's servant. Although the supernatural element is slight, this is a very good story.

"A Night on the Borders of the Black Forest" opens with two hikers meeting in Germany. They decide to proceed together and take shelter at a dubious looking farmhouse/inn where one of them is drugged. The protagonist realizes what has happened to his companion and anticipates an attack by the two brothers who run the inn. They thwart the attack and escape. The only supernatural element is that the drugged man has a vision of the previous murders perpetrated by the twosome that proves to be entirely accurate.

"A Service of Danger" is set during the Napoleonic wars. A small group of men are sent out to scout the enemy emplacements when their officer suspects a trap is being laid. The narrator sees them come back through the woods, but later discovers that all of them died in a battle shortly before he saw them. The battle sequences are well handled but the supernatural element is almost an afterthought.

"An Engineer's Story" is pretty minor. A man driven to revenge plans to wreck a train to kill the woman who provoked the fight in which he killed his best friend. At the last minute, the ghost of the friend appears and shuts down the engine. An artist becomes obsessed by a picture in "Cain" which portrays the title character just after the murder of Abel. He discovers that the artist who painted it shortly thereafter murdered his own brother, apparently under the influence of his creation.

"In the Confessional" is a fairly typical ghost story. A traveler visits a small German town where he sees what he believes to be a priest at the local church. The innkeeper where he stops tells him that their current priest took over when his brother was murdered by a man who impersonated him. The traveler then meets the priest, who is not the man he saw, and during the course of their conversation he realizes that he saw the ghost of the murderer, doomed to remain at the scene of his crimes.

"Love and Money" concerns a young German officer who has fallen in love but lacks the wealth required by his prospective father-in-law. Money begins to inexplicably appear in his room at intervals thereafter, which suggests the supernatural until we learn that he gambles in his sleep and has no conscious memory of it. The premise is absurd and the story is minor.

"My Brother's Ghost Story" is another standard ghost tale. A group of travelers become friends. One of them eventually leaves the group and a short time later his former companions experience cold spots, odd feelings of sadness, and one of them hears the music box that the missing man loved to play. They have a brief vision of him the following day, shortly before finding his dead body. He has been killed in an accident.

"Number Three" takes place at a pottery. A new expert has been hired and the longstanding employees resent him for his standing and his French nationality. Some believe that he has the evil eye. One of the men has been in love with a local girl and he is devastated when he learns that she has agreed to marry the Frenchman. A quarrel follows, off stage, which we only learn of through implication because the thwarted lover's ghost is seen on two occasions at the pottery, and his ashes are found inside one of the ovens. There is no proof so the Frenchman is released, but the romance comes to an end. "Sister Johanna's Story" is another very minor tale in which a man murders his brother for stealing his wife, then kills himself, only to appear briefly to the narrator.

"The Discovery of the Treasure Isles" is set in the middle of the 18th Century. It opens with an encounter between two merchant ships. The narrator is the captain of one of them, and he is intrigued when the other shows him a chart to two supposedly uninhabited islands where gold and jewels abound. His own hold is full of this cargo, which is a strong argument in favor of his story. The narrator decides to divert his ship to these islands, even though his crew insists that there is no land at those coordinates.

The islands are only intermittently visible and when the captain tries to row ashore, his boat is swamped and he is forced to swim for it. On land again, he finds some mysterious ruins. Wandering alone, he stumbles upon the wreckage of his own ship, which has clearly having been rotting on the beach for years even though he left it only a day earlier. There is no sign of the crew but he does find a manuscript written by his first mate, describing an illness that claimed them all – but it is dated several months after the day they arrived, which to the narrator was only yesterday. He takes the ship's lifeboat and leaves the island, never to be heard of again.

"The Eleventh of March" is another minor ghost story. A traveler encounters a monk whose appearance is unsettling, then visits the local monastery, where he learns that the monk in question committed some unnamed crime for which he lost his life. "The Recollections of Professor Henneberg" refer to his conviction that he has been reincarnated many times. The story consists of a long account that provides some evidence that he might be right, but it is tedious and wanders a great deal.

"The Four Fifteen Express" starts with an encounter on a train. The narrator strikes up a conversation with a casual acquaintance named John Dwerrihouse, who disappears mysteriously at one of the local stations. He mentions this to the people he is visiting, only to discover that Dwerrihouse vanished months earlier with funds he embezzled from his employer. The narrator also recovered a cigar case that Dwerrihouse dropped, and it is positively identified as his. Further investigation reveals that the missing man is dead, murdered by his partner in crime, who confesses when confronted. But the murder took place months earlier, so the narrator was witnessing an echo of the past.

"The Phantom Coach" is the author's best known story. The narrator is out hunting one wintry night when he loses his way. He takes shelter for a while at the house of a reclusive retired scientist, who tells him that he lost his reputation because he advocated some unmentioned field of knowledge that his peers considered mythical. This element of the story has no relevance to the rest. He then sets out to intercept the night mail coach and beg a ride home. Nine years earlier the previous night coach went over the edge of a cliff, killing all six passengers. A coach shows up and he is allowed to board, but within minutes he realizes that the other three passengers are dead and rotting, although they still move and their eyes are alert. The crash is repeated but this time someone survives, obviously the narrator, who is found in a snowdrift the following day but who never tells anyone the details of his experience.

"The Story of Salome" is another minor piece. A man meets a beautiful young woman in a graveyard. She asks him to say a prayer over a grave which he later discovers in her own. "Four Ghost Stories" is a collection of vignettes, all involving ghostly appearances but none particularly memorable.

"Was It an Illusion? A Parson's Story" involves a school inspector's visit to a remote English town. While walking cross country, he encounters a man who mysteriously disappears and spots a young boy, who seems to have sprung up out of nowhere. He encounters the same man when he reaches the town, but is told that this is impossible because he did not leave his home all of that evening. During a conversation, the inspector notices that the two men cast three separate shadows.

The local squire and landlord turns out to be an old friend of the inspector from Oxford and he is invited to stay at the manor house. While he is there, the local lake goes suddenly dry, apparently draining into an underground cavern. The inspector sees the young boy again, but his companion at the time insists that no one else was present. A boy's body is found in the mud of the lake bottom, evidently the victim of murder, and he is identified as a young relative of the local school master who had disappeared. The crime is thus revealed.

Edwards' short fiction is frequently told in the first person and many of them are set in Germany. She also varied from past tense to present tense narration within the same story at times, for no apparent reason. Her supernatural events are as likely to be as beneficial as harmful. The lack of real melodrama in most of her short stories probably accounts for their obscurity.

R. MURRAY GILCHRIST

Robert Murray Gilchrist (1868-1917) was a British novelist and short story writer who has achieved some belated critical acclaim but not enough to bring most of his work back into print. The exception is his short horror fiction, which seems likely to be the work for which he will be best remembered. Many of his stories are little more than vignettes, but he was often able to pack a considerable punch into just a comparatively few words.

Some of his stories resemble the fantastic adventures of Clark Ashton Smith and Lord Dunsany. "The Crimson Weaver," for example, concerns two travelers whose time and place are never explicitly defined. They ignore a warning from a crone and venture into a landscape that has not been seen by a human being in many years. They find a palace and are silently greeted by a woman wearing tattered crimson clothing. One of them is seduced by her and when the other attempts a rescue, he discovers that the woman is an inhuman thing that wears the lives of her victims.

"The Stone Dragon" has a more conventional setting. Ralph Eyre has never understood why his late father kept him from meeting his Aunt Barbara, but he knows that they quarreled when she tried to convince him to arrange a marriage between Ralph and one of her daughters. Seven years after his father's death, Barbara dies and her will requires him to marry one of her daughters in order to inherit her estate.

Eyre pays a visit to his cousins, Rachel and Mary, the first a stunning beauty, the second shy and unattractive. Rachel wears a pair of gloves that were fashioned from the skin of an executed murderess. He is determined to marry one of them and Rachel is confident that she will be his wife, but Ralph realizes that it is Mary whom he loves. The inevitable scene follows and Rachel attempts to kill Ralph, but wounds Mary instead, then vanishes. Months later, following the wedding, she returns, but is found dead shortly thereafter. There is a hint that she was already dead when she arrived, but it is never explicitly stated.

In "The Lover's Ordeal" a man agrees to spend a night in a supposedly haunted house. He encounters a mysterious woman there and discovers that the story of a haunting is a lie to cover up the fact that it is the lair of a vampire. Fortunately, he is saved at the last minute by the woman he loves.

"The Manuscript of Francis Shackerley" is very minor. The protagonist falls in love with the wife of a man known to have studied magic. They are discovered, she is killed, but he is ensorcelled in such a way that he cannot speak of these events until the magician has died. Similarly "Midsummer Madness" is both forgettable and tediously ambiguous. On the day of his wedding, a man discovers that his wife to be is either mad or is subject to a kind of spiritual possession.

"The Return" is a bland ghost story. A man who went abroad for twenty years in order to earn a fortune and marry the woman he loves returns and finds her very changed. But before that first night is over, he falls into a deep sleep, and when he wakens he learns that she committed suicide shortly after he left. "Dame Inowslad" is psychological horror rather than supernatural. A woman deserted by her lover keeps her dead baby as a reminder of her fall from grace. "Witch In-Grain" is a vignette about a woman falling prey to an ancient curse.

"The Basilisk" concerns a young woman who tells the man courting her that she is incapable of love, that she once encountered a basilisk that turned her inner self to stone. He initially believes this to be a metaphor, but eventually she decides to allow him to help her escape the spell that has been placed upon her. She leads him blindfolded into an unknown place where he catches a glimpse of the creature of mythology. The spell is broken and they return to the normal world, where he promptly falls dead. The ending is a bit problematic since the dead man is the narrator.

"The Grotto at Ravensdale" is a predictable ghost story. After catching sight of a mysterious figure which seems to vanish into thin air, a woman discovers that a previous resident of the area died in one of the caves after an unhappy love affair. She finds herself drawn to the cave as well and the story ends with her body being found lying within it.

The death of his last remaining relative brings a man home to England in "The Madness of Betty Hooton." Betty rejected his proposal forty years previously and he had gone abroad and made a fortune, never returning during that period. Shortly after arriving he learns that she went quietly mad when he left and has been cared for by her unmarried sister ever since. He goes to see her but she insists that she died when he left. This one is more psychological suspense than horror, although it does build some reasonable tension.

A musician conjures up an authentic glimpse of Hell in "The Priest's Pavan." A man seeks shelter after becoming lost on the moors in "A Night on the Moor." Another traveler leads him to a great hall in the wilderness and he is entertained by the residents, but in the morning he finds himself inexplicably outdoors again. He asks about the hall and discovers that it fell into ruins many years earlier. "The Pageant of Ghosts" is a vignette in which a man sees a ghostly procession. "A Witch in the Peak" is another ambiguous tale whrein a man believes he has confronted a witch, though she denies it.

The rest of Gilchrist's stories are non-fantastic, occasionally humorous, sometimes romantic, although his lovers generally end up separated. "Dryas and Lady Greenleaf" hints at magic but is ambiguous. Gilchrist was a minor writer and none of his shorts are memorable. He was particularly bad at endings, and a good many of these have no real climax or resolution.

W.W. JACOBS

William Wymark Jacobs (1863-1943) was a British writer noted at the time for his humorous fiction, although he is best remembered now for "The Monkey's Paw", possibly the best known horror short story not written by Edgar Allan Poe. Much of his work had maritime themes and settings. He turned to full time writing in his thirties with great relief, having no interest in ordinary jobs.

"The Monkey's Paw" is the ultimate tale of "be careful what you wish for." The White family – a couple and their grown son – are entertained by the Sergeant Major, a retired traveler who shows them a mummified mummy's paw supposedly created by a fakir in India. The fakir purportedly "wanted to show that fate ruled people's lives, and that those who interfered with it did so to their sorrow." The paw was designed to give three separate men three wishes. The first man used his final wish to kill himself. The Sergeant Major has had three wishes, but is unwilling to talk about them.

The Sergeant Major throws the paw onto the fire but it is rescued by the Whites. The father takes possession, but then announces that he cannot think of anything to wish for because he has everything he needs. He finally wishes for a small sum of money, not really taking it seriously, but the paw seems to move in his hand and all three of the Whites feel a sense of impending danger.

The following day their son goes off to work. A few hours later a representative of the company arrives to tell them their son fell into the machinery and is dead. He offers compensation that is the exact amount that the elder White wished for. Then days later, at his wife's urging, he wishes their son were alive again. There is a knocking at the door in the night and before the wife can open it, her husband – knowing that their son was mangled and decayed, wishes him back into the grave. The story is very short and very efficiently delivers its three part climax.

"The Well" is also quite effective. Wilfred tries to blackmail his cousin Jem and promptly disappears. The suggestion is quite clear that he has been murdered to ensure his silence. Some weeks later Jem and his new wife are walking the grounds when she goes to sit by a disused well, despite his suggestion that they go elsewhere. She fancies that she hears someone calling for help and accidentally drops a valuable bracelet into the well, then insists that he recover it. The next day he attempts to fish it out with a hook but fails. He arranges to have himself lowered into the well, but something happens which alarms his servants. They pull up the rope and find it wrapped around the dead body of the missing man with Jem holding onto it. He loses his grip and falls back into the water, now dead as well. There is no mystery about where Wilfred's body has been but the suspense leading up to its recovery is skillfully developed.

"The Three Sisters" opens with the death of the oldest of three spinsters, who has promised to return to lead each of the others to the afterlife when their time has come. One of the two survivors becomes such a miser that the other begins to be afraid of her. There are also hints that there is another presence in the house, particularly in the locked room where the first sister died. The miser impersonates the dead sister and scares the third to death one night. She is then frightened to death herself, either by a guilty illusion or by the returned presence of her oldest sister.

Four young men decide to spend a night in a haunted house in "The Toll-House," despite reports of frequent deaths among people who visit the premises. Three of them fall asleep and the fourth is hounded through the house by strange sounds and eventually falls to his death. Although quite short, this is a very powerful story that develops quickly and has a strong climax.

"Jerry Bundler" is a sort of ghost story. A group of men at an inn are spooked by stories of the local ghost, and when one of them impersonates the apparition, he is fatally shot by another. "His Brother's Keeper" is more psychological. A man kills an acquaintance and buries him in the garden, but at night he sleepwalks and begins to disinter the body. "The Lost Ship" is not really horror but has the feel of the genre. Years after a ship disappears at sea, one member of the crew returns, so exhausted that he cannot speak coherently. He promises to tell his story and clear up the mystery on the following morning, but dies in his sleep.

"The Brown Man's Servant" is quite long for Jacobs. A pawnbroker buys a stolen diamond from a disreputable sailor, who tells him that he is on the run from his former partners, one of whom is Burmese. The sailor is murdered and the pawnbroker receives open threats that he will die as well if he does not return the diamond, that he will die at the hands of a devil. To illustrate the point, the Burmese tells him that he has already cursed the pawnbroker's cat. The cat dies mysteriously and that night there are sounds of something moving in the shop after the lights are out. It is a poisonous snake rather than anything supernatural, and it fulfills its mission.

"Over the Side" features what the crew of a ship believes to be a man returned from the dead, but the explanation is perfectly rational. "The Vigil" involves a haunting, but the ghosts are all fake. Another fake apparition appears in "Sam's Ghost." There is a genuine vision in "In Mid-Atlantic," but the story is humorous and the fantastic content is peripheral. Similarly there is clairvoyance in "The Castaway" but no actual supernatural danger.

Jacobs was a very skilled short story writer and quite a large number of his non-fantastic stories involve elements of mystery. A surprisingly large number of them are quite entertaining and most hold up very well. His substantial body of work deserves to be better known, but it is almost certain that he will always be remembered as the man who wrote "The Monkey's Paw" and for little else.

EDITH NESBIT

Edith Nesbit (1858-1924) was a British novelist best known for her forty books for children. She was a political activist and socialist, a follower of William Morris and a member of the Fabian society. Although Nesbit wrote no horror novels, she did write for adults as well and a number of her short stories involved the supernatural.

"Man-Size in Marble" is her best known horror tale. A man and his wife, painter and writer respectively, move into a small cottage in a remote town. Their only servant is a local woman who regales them with tales of local legends, until one day she mysteriously gives notice. The husband inquires further and the woman admits that she would be willing to come back after a week, but not until after All Saints' Eve. Local legend has it that two life sized stone statues in the local church walk abroad on that night and return to their home, which is where the couple currently resides.

The husband is skeptical and on the night in question he leaves his wife sleeping, fails to lock the door, and walks to the church, where he discovers that the two statues are missing. He runs out in panic and into the arms of the local doctor, who insists that he is mistaken. They return to the church and the statues are in place, but the hand of one of them is broken. When he returns to his home, he finds his wife dead, one hand clutching a single marble finger broken from its original place.

"Uncle Abraham's Romance" is a very brief ghost story. An elderly man recounts his romantic meetings with a young woman at the local cemetery, until he discovers she died a century earlier. "John Charrington's Wedding" is quite grim. A young man promises to marry his fiancé even if he has to come back from the dead. On the day of the wedding, he appears pale and disoriented, but the wedding is completed and the two leave in a carriage. But when it arrives at its destination, he is gone and the bride is in a coma which will eventually prove fatal. It is only then that we learn that he died hours before the wedding – although the story telegraphs its ending very clearly.

"From the Dead" opens with a complicated lovers' quadrangle. The narrator, Arthur Marsh, is engaged to Elvira, who is actually in love with Oscar Helmont. Oscar's sister Ida is in love with the narrator. She brings him a letter supposedly written by Elvira, proclaiming her love for Oscar, and he sends a letter releasing her from the engagement. But Ida later admits that she forged the letter in order to enhance her own chances, and in fact she and Arthur are now married.

Enraged by the revelation, he announces that she has ruined his life and walks out of their house. Within hours he regrets his behavior and returns, but she has gone and a subsequent search finds no trace of her, although there is a suggestion that she has thrown herself from a cliff into the sea. Months later he receives a telegram that she is dying in a distant village. He rushes there only to find that she has just died, and that she has had his child. That night he prays wildly for her to return and forgive him, and during the night her corpse visits him in his room in an effectively creepy sequence.

The protagonist of "The Three Drugs" is set upon by thieves one night and finds shelter in the house of a man who turns out to be a mad scientist. The scientist is experimenting with drugs which are designed to create a superhuman and he has a room full of dead people who succumbed to its side effects. He binds his new subject who seems to have received only beneficial effects from the drugs, then administers them to himself. Unfortunately, he becomes paralyzed and cannot take the third drug, which means his death, and the protagonist could not help even if he wanted to. The story is rather overwrought as the characters make long speeches to one another.

"The Violet Car" opens with the arrival of a nurse at a remote farm. She has been hired to help the wife of an elderly man whom he believes to be unbalanced, although the form of her delusion is supposedly that she thinks that he is the one who is mad. The nurse likes them both but comes to feel that they are caught up in a pervasive fear, the cause of which is a complete mystery to her.

The wife tells her that her husband sees, hears, and smells things which are not perceptible to anyone else and that it all began when their daughter was fatally injured by a violet automobile. The car and its driver went over a cliff a short time later. It subsequently is revealed that her employer misdirected the driver intentionally, enraged by his daughter's death. The nurse finally sees the car herself, just as the old man throws himself in front of it. Although the doctor insists that he died of heart failure, she knows that he was killed by the phantom car. This is a very fine story, economically told and with a strongly developed atmosphere.

"The Pavilion" involves a cursed place, a pavilion where people who sleep there sometimes die and where dead animals can be found with surprising frequency. All of the people who died had strange small wounds on their body, with no apparent cause. A young man agrees to spend part of a night there on a dare and he is found dead. The vines that cover part of the pavilion have come inside and killed him. This is another excellent story.

"Hurst of Hurstcote" is ambiguous. A man believes that his wife's soul is trapped in her body and cannot leave until he too is dead. The protagonist assumes that his friend has gone mad with grief, but ever afterward he wonders whether or not he was right. "In the Dark" is an odd story about a man who believes that duplicates of the body of someone he murdered keep appearing near him on the anniversary of the crime, and in fact at the end, multiple bodies are found. But they are all different men. The explanation is psychological but there is an implication that something supernatural was involved as well.

"The Head" is not fantastic at all. A madman who lost the woman he loved in a fire and blames the man she married builds a replica of that event, and eventually includes the man's real head as part of the exhibit. "The Mystery of the Semi-Detached" is a vignette about a man who has a prescient vision of a murder. "The Ebony Frame" is an uninteresting story about a ghost that steps out of a painting.

"The Five Senses" seems quite modern. Dr. Boyd Thompson is a scientist who has developed a number of worthwhile treatments for human beings partly as a result of his experimental dissections of animals. His fiancé breaks things off because she cannot bear the thought of vivisection. Then he tests an experimental drug on himself and falls into a coma so deep that he is about to be buried when he finally wakens. Inexplicably this convinces him to give up scientific research in a rather muddled conclusion.

"The Shadow" is a haunted house story without ghosts. The couple living there are its first residents so there can be no gloomy history to be unearthed. She seems oblivious but he feels as though something follows him in the passageways and that it all originates with one particular cupboard. A friend comes to stay with them and she experiences the same sensations, even sees an apparently sentient shadow that moves of its own volition. It is the shadow of death, and it claims three lives by the end of a reasonably good story.

"The Power of Darkness" is another psychological tale. A man takes a bet that he can't spend a night in a waxwork museum, and he goes insane when one of the figures – actually another man who fell asleep – moves in the darkness. There is nothing supernatural in "The Haunted Inheritance" either, but both characters believe the other to be a ghost until late in the story. "Number 17" is about a haunted room, but it turns out to be a hoax. "The Letter in Brown Ink" is explained as madness. "The Haunted House" is actually inhabited by a mad scientist. "The Detective" is another minor, low key ghost story.

Nesbit's supernatural fiction is little more than a footnote to her career, but it is an important footnote because it demonstrates the diverse quality of her writing talents and because several of the stories hold up well and should be read today.